*Library Media Skills*

*TEACHING LIBRARY MEDIA RESEARCH AND INFORMATION SKILLS SERIES*

Edited by Paula Kay Montgomery

**Library Media Skills: Strategies for Instructing Primary Students.** By Alice R. Seaver.

**Media Skills for Middle Schools: Strategies for Library Media Specialists and Teachers.** By Lucille W. Van Vliet.

**Ready for Reference: Media Skills for Intermediate Students.** By Barbara Bradley Zlotnick.

# LIBRARY MEDIA SKILLS

## Strategies for
## Instructing Primary Students

## ALICE R. SEAVER

EDITED BY
**PAULA KAY MONTGOMERY**

1984
Libraries Unlimited, Inc.
Littleton, Colorado

LIBRARIES UNLIMITED, INC.
P.O. Box 263
Littleton, Colorado 80160-0263

**Library of Congress Cataloging in Publication Data**

Seaver, Alice R., 1940-
    Library media skills.

    (Teaching library media research and information
skills series)
    Includes index.
    1. Instructional materials centers--User education.
2. School children--Library orientation. 3. School
libraries (Elementary school)--Activity programs.
4. Media programs (Education) I. Title. II. Series.
Z675.S3S418   1984   025.5'678222   84-965
ISBN 0-87287-409-5 (pbk.)

Libraries Unlimited books are bound with Type II nonwoven material that meets and exceeds National Association of State Textbook Administrators' Type II nonwoven material specifications Class A through E.

# *Table of Contents*

# *List of Illustrations*

# *Foreword*

One of the more precious gifts that teachers can give to students is the set of skills required to search for, use, comprehend, and evaluate information within their environment. It is in the early grades that students begin to develop these information skills. The simple joy of wanting to know seen in most young children when they enter school is not to be wasted. Too often, this joy loses its sparkle.

*Library Media Skills: Strategies for Instructing Primary Students* is the first in the series *Teaching Library Media Research and Information Skills.* It focuses on a simple but realistic process for the school library media specialist to plan with the classroom teacher for library media skills instruction. It combines a description of the process for instruction with practical suggestions for activities for use with young students. Special emphasis has been given to more individualized or small group approaches. The intent is not to provide all the activities needed in a year, but to suggest some rational methods for working with young students in a way that will be meaningful for them.

The author, Alice R. Seaver, an experienced library media specialist and teacher for ten years, developed her strategies while working in an elementary school in Montgomery County Public Schools in Gaithersburg, Maryland. She has shared informally her discussion techniques, lap packs, and learning centers with her colleagues during those years. All the units in this book have been used successfully with students.

Part I identifies the process in implementing a program with primary grade students. Part II provides seven models of activities described in Part I that may be copied or adapted.

Both the author and series editor hope that school library media specialists and classroom teachers will find this book helpful in planning their programs.

Paula Kay Montgomery

# *Preface*

*Library Media Skills: Strategies for Instructing Primary Students* has two major goals:

1.  To provide future and practicing school library media specialists with strategies for teaching primary students the skills needed to use the library media center efficiently and effectively.

2.  To provide some practical suggestions that can make the library media specialist's task easier and more effective.

The task of the school library media specialist has changed dramatically from the traditional role of keeper and dispenser of books to the role of a key person on the instructional staff of the elementary school. Not only is today's library media specialist tasked with acquisitions and organization of materials, but he or she is also tasked with providing instruction on locating, selecting, utilizing, and producing various media. Today's media includes not only the books of yesterday's library, but also the films, filmstrips, realia, charts, video tape equipment, and computer hardware and software of today's library media center.

The need exists for practical ways to help the library media specialist meet the new demands of this ever changing role. As there are few sources of guidance or assistance, this book will be of value to practicing and future school library media specialists. *Library Media Skills: Strategies for Instructing Primary Students* is designed to provide guides and models for planning and implementing a program of instruction for primary students from headstart and kindergarten to third grade. It does not attempt to address all the problems or tasks of the school library media specialist, but it does offer guidance through practical suggestions that can be used or modified. This book provides working models that can be used as springboards for giving primary students a library media skills program that will prepare them for the additional and refined skills expected of them in later school years.

Part I, comprising the first six chapters, outlines the processes and techniques required to meet the instructional needs of primary students. The underlying philosophy is that such needs can be best met by a systematic approach which includes the identification of objectives and prerequisite skills, the use of various instructional strategies and materials, and the continual evaluation of the total instructional program. Specific techniques are given for accomplishing identified objectives. Grouping considerations for instruction; rewarding student accomplishments; literature enrichment and awareness; evaluation of student learnings, materials and instruction; and, methods of record keeping are included in the first six chapters. The first chapter in Part II, chapter 7, provides suggestions for creating and storing learning materials. Chapter 8 contains sample learning activities which can be used as models for providing primary students with a library media skills program that will prepare them for the additional and refined skills expected of them in later years.

# Part I

# 1  *Implementation of a Library Media Skills Program*

Implementation of a library media skills program that meets student needs must combine a cooperative systematic approach with realistic expectations. A cooperative systematic approach is one in which the classroom teacher and the library media specialist together plan an instructional program for students that integrates subject area curriculum objectives with library media skills objectives. Additionally, the cooperative systematic approach includes a process in which the classroom teacher and the library media specialist consider

- objectives

- prerequisite skills

- instructional strategies and materials

- evaluation and assessment

One must have realistic expectations for accomplishing all the tasks that are required of the library media specialist. It must be realized that the implementation of a library media skills program is only one of those tasks. Being familiar with the objectives of the subject area curriculum, being responsible for acquisition of new materials that support the curriculum and are of interest to students, providing support for the entire teaching staff, keeping accurate records of materials and equipment, keeping the collection of materials up-to-date by weeding and acquisition, assisting students and staff in locating and borrowing needed materials, keeping informed as to what materials are being published and produced, seeing that equipment is operational, and attending to the many other responsibilities of operating a library media center are essential, since these activities support and work in concert with the total school instructional program. The library media specialist's task is enormous, but the keys to success include: (1) planning, (2) assessing present practices for effectiveness and efficiency, (3) working toward goals in small steps, (4) adding to what is already available or happening, (5) getting involvement and assistance from others, and (6) realizing the limitations of being human.

An evaluation of the total instructional program and use of time by the classroom teacher, students, and library media specialist should be a component of the implementation process. Some of the present practices and instructional methods may not be efficient in terms of the amount of time engaged in learning compared to the amount of learning. The student groupings, type of material(s), method, and vehicle for instruction may need to be modified. The library media specialist needs to examine how library media skills are being taught. Are library media skills being taught as a result of cooperative planning between library media specialist and the classroom teacher? Are library media skills objectives and subject area curriculum objectives being integrated into activities that are designed to meet the objectives for both? Is the instruction of library media skills the sole responsibility of the library media specialist? In response to these questions, the classroom teacher and the library media specialist have two major tasks in implementing a program of instruction: (1) planning and instructing and (2) creating or providing learning materials that will support the program of instruction.

## PLANNING AND INSTRUCTION

The first step in planning is to assess the present program of instruction. Ideally, the planning should be a cooperative effort between the classroom teacher and the library media specialist. If it is not, this may be a place to start. To initiate such a plan, it will be necessary to determine what is happening in the school and to approach the principal for support. If the principal is not supportive of an integrated approach, all is not lost. If one teacher can be enlisted to try a flexible approach to library media skills instruction that would include joint planning and teaming for instruction, the library media skills program can move forward.

If the principal is cooperative, the next step would be to present the integrated approach to teaching library media skills instruction to the entire staff. Sample instructional plans might be presented.

An integrated approach with joint planning, teaming for instruction, and flexible scheduling with one or two teachers would be a reasonable start. The goal for each succeeding year might be to enlist one or two classroom teachers to work cooperatively with the library media specialist.

## CREATING LEARNING MATERIALS

Taking stock of materials already available for instruction is an important step in implementing a program. Library media skills objectives may need to be listed according to grade level. The library media specialist may provide a notation next to each objective: (1) materials available and accessible, (2) appropriate student groupings for that material, and (3) effectiveness of the material. Once this task has been completed, a list of materials or instructional plans needed to meet objectives can be generated. Then the list can be put in a tentative order of priority—with the understanding that this list can and should be revised as instructional needs and other factors change.

Although the sight of the generated list may be overwhelming, it represents a major task that has been completed. The task of planning and preparing for a library media skills program for students can now be developed and modified. Working through this process in small steps will get the job done. Getting ideas from other people or using materials and ideas that are already available or can be borrowed as models can save much time. For example, if a learning material on the use of a dictionary for second-grade students is available, a similar set could be made for older students by such modifications as a new central theme, additional skills, or a different format. The framework is already there.

Getting assistance from others can save time. This assistance can take many forms. Learning materials and instructional ideas shared by other classroom teachers and library media specialists is one way. It is easier to adapt materials or instructional ideas for the individual school situation than to start from scratch. A "swap meet" to share ideas with other library media specialists who work nearby may be planned. Most library media specialists are proficient in specialized areas of library media skills. These resources should be tapped. Some of the most exciting and useful meetings are those in which people with similar problems and tasks get together and share how they solve problems or how they accomplish tasks. One library media specialist may have an easy and effective way of teaching young students how to make animated films, while another may be talented at creating learning centers. Those talents should be shared to make the job easier. Parents or senior citizens can provide many useful services. These services can take such varied forms as typing masters of learning materials; replacing worn materials; and providing another hand for taking dictation of sentences, paragraphs, or stories for student-made books. Older students can also be pressed into service. They feel useful, learn from such experiences, and enjoy helping. They may enjoy coloring, cutting out letters, or doing similar tasks. Artistically talented students may be able to provide illustrations or graphics for learning materials.

Planning and creating learning materials with classroom teachers is another possibility. Providing the instruction for a library media skill objective is not necessarily the sole responsibility of the library media specialist. When the library media specialist and the classroom teacher are examining library media skills objectives, they may find that some objectives seem to fit into the classroom teacher's activity. The classroom teacher may decide to teach a particular skill or skills that would be appropriate to what is being taught in the classroom. Another approach might be for the library media specialist to provide the learning materials. Then the students would complete the work and the classroom teacher would be responsible for providing needed assistance and for evaluating students' work. Any number of plans for sharing the instructional responsibilities could be conceived.

Another possibility for ideas and assistance is the involvement of a subject specialist. This may be particularly useful when new curriculum is developed. For example, the social studies specialist may be able to provide assistance with knowledge of commercially prepared materials that would be useful in teaching or reviewing library media skills objectives that deal with the use of almanacs or atlases. These specialists may be able to provide valuable assistance or materials.

Today's world is hectic and full of pressure. Unnecessary stresses should not be added to those that cannot be avoided. The library media specialist needs to realize that students and classroom teachers want to feel good about themselves. Whenever a task arises, the library media specialist should consider who else could do the task or who would be able to provide assistance. The involvement of students and teachers can add to their sense of accomplishment and happiness with the program. The message is: Everything does not have to be and should not be done by the library media specialist.

In summary, library media skills instruction is a cooperative, systematic approach in which the classroom teacher and the library media specialist set objectives, determine prerequisite skills, identify and use instructional strategies and materials, and evaluate student achievement in the program.

## BIBLIOGRAPHY

Walker, H. Thomas, and Paula Kay Montgomery. *Teaching Library Media Skills.* 2d ed. Littleton, Colo.: Libraries Unlimited, Inc., 1983.

Wehmeyer, Lillian Biermann. *The School Librarian as Educator.* Littleton, Colo.: Libraries Unlimited, Inc., 1976.

# 2

# *Program*
# *Planning*

The classroom teacher and the library media specialist's major instructional tasks are to help students learn to obtain information independently and to provide them with the skills that will enable them to learn. Implementing an instructional program to teach primary students the library media skills that are necessary for them to develop into information-seeking citizens is a difficult task, but a well-developed plan can eliminate much time and effort. Some of the issues that need to be addressed to implement such a plan are

- What do the students need to learn?

- What objectives need to be taught?

- What strategies are appropriate to teach those objectives?

- What methods and materials can be used?

- How can the plan be implemented?

## COOPERATIVE PLANNING

Ideally, the planning should be a cooperative effort between the classroom teacher and the library media specialist. This type of planning should be a goal. Realistically, this may not happen immediately in some schools or school systems. The library media specialist needs administrative support. The school principal needs to be committed to this philosophy. However, if the principal is not supportive of this planning strategy, such planning can still be initiated. One cooperative classroom teacher is a start.

## PLANNING SESSIONS

Prior to the first planning session, both the classroom teacher and the library media specialist need to make preparations.

## Preplanning

The preplanning for the library media specialist should include (1) providing the classroom teacher with a preplanning sheet (see figures 2.1 and 2.2, Planning Resource Sheets #1 and #2, respectively, see pages 8 and 9) and library media skills and objectives and (2) reviewing the units of study and objectives for social studies, science, and language arts.

The preplanning for the classroom teacher should include (1) filling out the preplanning sheet and (2) reviewing library media skills objectives.

## Long-Term Planning

During the first planning session, the classroom teacher and the library media specialist should lay out a global plan for the year. They should use the preplanning sheet (fig. 2.1, see page 8), list subject area objectives and guides and library media skills objectives, and match subject area curriculum with library media skills in broad terms. Figure 2.2 (see page 9) shows a planning sheet that has been completed as a sample of a broad year's plan.

A further illustration of this process may be helpful. A third grade teacher is planning a unit on magnets for the end of September and most of October. Prerequisite library media skills might require students to be able to: (1) locate trade books and encyclopedias and (2) utilize those resources to locate information.

Long-term planning could include matching units of study with a few library media skills as objectives. Here is an example.

### Third Grade

|  | Curriculum Units | Library Media Skills |
|---|---|---|
| September | Map skills | Make map of library media center |
|  | Magnets | Locate books on magnets Use trade books and encyclopedias to locate information |

Any written plans should be duplicated so that the classroom teacher and the library media specialist each have a copy.

## Short-Term Planning

Short-term plans should cover at least six weeks of instruction. Modifications can be made as needed. For short-term planning, the classroom teacher and library media specialist need to determine

1. What prerequisite library media skills are needed

2. What activities will help students acquire needed skills

3. Who will be responsible for instruction

4. When students will receive instruction (schedule)

5. What materials will be used

(Text continues on page 10.)

PREPLANNING SHEET

Teacher:
Grade Level:

| | Social Studies Units | Science Units | Language Arts Units |
|---|---|---|---|
| SEPT. | | | |
| OCT. | | | |
| NOV. | | | |
| DEC. | | | |
| JAN. | | | |
| FEB. | | | |
| MAR. | | | |
| APR. | | | |
| MAY | | | |
| JUNE | | | |

Support needed:
Bibliographies:
Order films:
Interlibrary loans:
Other:

Fig. 2.1. Planning Resource Sheet #1, a preplanning sheet.

PREPLANNING SHEET

Teacher: Martha Anderson
Grade Level: third

| Social Studies Units | Science Units | Language Arts Units |
|---|---|---|
| | | |
| SEPT. | | Diaries/Assessments |
| Getting along | Energy | Punctuation/Sentences |
| Map skills | | Language use |
| OCT. | | |
| Local community | Matter | Folktales * |
| NOV. | | |
| | | Letter writing |
| DEC. | Living things * | |
| Washington, D.C. | | Poetry* |
| JAN. | | |
| | | Writing stories |
| FEB. | Living things/ | Report writing |
| Japan* | Environment | |
| MAR. | | |
| Mexico * | Universe in | |
| APR. | Change * | |
| MAY | | |
| JUNE | | |

Support Needed:
Bibliographies: *items
Order films: all units as needed

Interlibrary loans: Report writing kit from
Rosedale Elem.
Other: Any local poets?

Fig. 2.2. Planning Resource Sheet #2, a sample of a completed preplanning sheet.

In order to determine what prerequisite library media skills are needed, the classroom teacher and the library media specialist may examine the objectives for the particular curriculum unit of study and the activities that will accomplish these objectives. Once a list of activities is generated, each activity needs to be reviewed to determine what library media skills are necessary for students to be successful. Planning Resource Sheet #3 (fig. 2.3) can be duplicated and used at this stage for short-term planning. Planning Resource Sheet #4 (fig. 2.4, see page 12) has been completed as a sample of a short-term planning sheet.

Next, the decision must be made as to who will be responsible for teaching the library media skills. The library media specialist may not always be responsible for such instruction. What follows are three examples of how the teaching responsibilities might be divided.

One, if the classroom teacher is doing a unit of study on reading and constructing maps, the library media specialist may not be the instructor for drawing a map of the library media center. The library media specialist's role may be to (1) schedule time for the class to come to the library media center to draw the map, and (2) provide an outline map of the library media center for the teacher to use.

Two, the classroom teacher and the library media specialist may decide to team teach a unit of study on the use of the encyclopedia to locate information about magnets. They may plan the instructional activities together as well as share the instructional responsibilities.

Three, in the same unit on magnets, the library media specialist may be responsible for providing the instructional materials and the instruction for use of the card catalog and locating resources (books and encyclopedias that have information on magnets).

Scheduling instruction and use of the library media center can be done in a variety of ways depending on the activities and the needs of the students. Students can be grouped for instruction in the following ways:

1. *Whole class.* For an introductory lesson, it might be appropriate to show a film on the use of encyclopedias. This could be done in either the classroom or the library media center.

2. *Small groups.* Students learning to use the card catalog could be scheduled for five or more periods of instruction over a period of a week or more. A class of students may be divided into groups to create a video tape program. Each committee may need instruction in production techniques and would be responsible for their part in the total production.

3. *Individual students.* New students or students who are not able to perform a particular skill might go to the library media center for instruction with another group for independent study. Students who are gifted might be scheduled to come to the library media center for independent study.

Materials to be used can be noted on the same short-term planning sheet (fig. 2.4, see page 12). It is to be hoped that a variety of resources, including human, will be utilized. Information about student groupings, instructional responsibilities, and supports needed may be listed on the short-term planning sheet. This part of the resource sheet may or may not be completed at the first short-term planning session. In fact, planning may require several sessions.

## Daily Planning

The next step is to plan and schedule daily activities using a blank calendar (see figures 2.5 and 2.6, Planning Resource Sheets #5 and #6, respectively; see pages 13 and 14) or a plan book. The resource sheets can be used for scheduling daily activities for one month at a time. For economy of space, abbreviations or symbols can be used on the resource sheets. Figure 2.6, which is a sample of a completed daily planning sheet, uses the following symbols: FS=Filmstrips; GT= Gifted and Talented Students; LA=Language Arts; LMS=Library Media Specialist; MU=Music; PA=Physical Activity; SC=Science; SS=Social Studies; and Resource=Numbered sheets that have detailed/additional information.

On this daily planning sheet, the following notes can be made: activity title, times, who is responsible for instruction, grouping, and materials. It may be useful to draw a box using a colored marker around the activities that the library media specialist is responsible for.

SHORT TERM PLANNING SHEET

Teacher:
Unit of Study:

Activity:

| Library Media Skills | Student Groupings | Materials | Responsibility | Support Needs |
|---|---|---|---|---|
| | | | | |

Activity:

| Library Media Skills | Student Groupings | Materials | Responsibility | Support Needs |
|---|---|---|---|---|
| | | | | |

Activity:

| Library Media Skills | Student Groupings | Materials | Responsibility | Support Needs |
|---|---|---|---|---|
| | | | | |

**Fig. 2.3. Planning Resource Sheet #3, a short-term planning sheet.**

Teacher: Martha Anderson
Unit of Study: Mexico

SHORT-TERM PLANNING SHEET

| Activity: Identify geographic characteristics of Mexico | | | | |
|---|---|---|---|---|
| Library Media Skills | Student Groupings | Materials | Responsibility | Support Needs |
| Locate specific maps using index<br><br>Identify specific map (geographic characteristics)<br><br>Use a simple atlas | Whole class: review needed vocabulary (geographic terms)<br><br>Small group: Jane, Tom, Steve, and Elizabeth need help using index | Outline map of Mexico<br><br>Kit: "Maps Show the Earth" Nystrom<br><br>My First Atlas<br><br>Wall map of Mexico | Teacher: all but small group<br><br>Library Media Specialist: work with small group | Outline map and student copies of My First Atlas from Library Media Specialist |

| Activity: Construct a relief map of Mexico | | | | |
|---|---|---|---|---|
| Library Media Skills | Student Groupings | Materials | Responsibility | Support Needs |
| Identify special map (geographic characteristics)<br><br>Use a simple atlas | Whole class: each student will make a model. | My First Atlas<br><br>Outline map<br><br>Modeling dough | Classroom teacher -- colors to show altitude and finish project<br><br>Art teacher -- intro. how to construct | Art teacher -- modeling dough<br><br>Library Media Specialist -- outline map showing altitude |

| Activity: Research Information on Mexican flag -- colors, symbols | | | | |
|---|---|---|---|---|
| Library Media Skills | Student Groupings | Materials | Responsibility | Support Needs |
| Use card catalog to locate trade books on Mexico<br><br>Locate books on Mexico<br><br>Locate information using encyclopedia and trade books | Small group: Dorothy K. Ken L. Christy S. | Encyclopedias<br><br>Trade books on Mexico<br><br>Task card | Library Media Specialist | None |

Fig. 2.4. Planning Resource Sheet #4, a sample of a completed short-term planning sheet.

DAILY PLANNING SHEET   MONTH:

Teacher:
Unit of Study:

| Monday | Tuesday | Wednesday | Thursday | Friday |
|--------|---------|-----------|----------|--------|
|        |         |           |          |        |
|        |         |           |          |        |
|        |         |           |          |        |
|        |         |           |          |        |

**Fig. 2.5. Planning Resource Sheet #5**, a daily planning sheet.

Teacher: Martha Anderson
Unit of Study: Mexico

DAILY PLANNING SHEET  MONTH: May

| Monday | Tuesday | Wednesday | Thursday | Friday |
|---|---|---|---|---|
|  | LA Intro geographic terms<br><br>SS Use kit "Maps" Show Symbols and geographic terms and Resource #1 | SS Use wall map and overhead transparencies — ask students questions (on Resource #2) | SS Use wall map Students will label their outline map (List on Mexico ditto #1) | PA Using compass and directions, students to locate objects on playground<br><br>SS Activity for film #7031 |
| Art Construct relief map<br><br>SS Finish relief map | Review map skills | Assessment of map skills | Group Work 1. LMS- flag research group 10:15  2. Flag construction  3. Open air market characteristics | Cont. Thurs. Activities Review map skills with those students who need help<br><br>Room mothers- assist with making enchiladas |
| LA Project presentation skills review<br><br>SS- Share research findings | LMS- GT students to research rain/dry season 1:30<br><br>SC experiment to show effect of material color on body temperature | SS Use Kit "four Biomes -- Rain Forest" use Resource #3 for discussion | LMS- GT research industry from forest to produce mural 10:15<br><br>SS Students hypothesize how vegetation regions help people | SS Students make chart of 4 veg. regions. Use Resource #4<br><br>LMS - cont. from Thurs. 9:00 |
| SS Groups to research: 1. animals/domestic 2. animals/wild<br><br>LA Team with LMS for index instruction 8:30 | MU Listen to cowboy songs for words/phrases from Mexican culture<br><br>SS Cont. from Monday | LA Vocab. for SS (Use Resource #5)<br><br>SS Discussion questions on water distribution (Resource #6) | Small Groups: research on vegetation of Mexico (Resource #7 for topics)<br><br>LMS special needs group topic "farm crops" 9:00 | SS Cont. Thurs. activity<br><br>LMS 10:15<br><br>Room mothers- assist with making churros |
| Art Using pastels students make drawing of vegetation<br><br>SS Share findings from Th. and F. | SS Discussion activities Use Resource #8 for questions<br><br>SC Test various soils for water retention | PA Mexican Hat Dance<br><br>SS Use f.s. "A World Nearby: Mexico" Pt. 2 List char. of family life. |  |  |

Fig. 2.6. Planning Resource Sheet #6, a sample of a completed daily planning sheet.

In summary, planning needs to be a cooperative effort between the classroom teacher and the library media specialist. This type of planning provides for more meaningful instruction for the students. Combining subject area objectives and library media skills objectives enables the student to learn library media skills through curriculum rather than in isolation. The model resource sheets are intended to be modified and adapted to the individual needs of the students, the classroom teachers, and the library media specialist.

## BIBLIOGRAPHY

Cagne, Robert M. *Essentials of Learning for Instruction.* Hinsdale, Ill.: The Dryden Press, 1975.

Condit, Martha O. "If Only the Teacher Had Stayed with the Class." *Elementary English* 52: (May 1975): 664-66.

Walker, H. Thomas, and Paula Kay Montgomery. *Teaching Library Media Skills.* 2d ed. Littleton, Colo.: Libraries Unlimited, Inc., 1983.

Wehmeyer, Lillian Biermann. *The School Librarian as Educator.* Littleton, Colo.: Libraries Unlimited, Inc., 1976.

# 3       *Identification of Objectives*

In the past, educational learning requirements were written in generalities that were difficult to measure or test. In keeping with present educational practices, objectives for this book are limited to behavioral objectives. Behavioral objectives are those objectives that are written in terms of student behavior that can be observed and measured.

An example of an objective written in general terms is as follows: The student will understand the elements of folktales. With this objective there is no expected behavior that can be concretely observed.

An example of a behavioral objective closely related to this generality is the following: After listening to and/or reading a folktale, the student will be able to select from a list the elements of a folktale that were present in that particular folktale.

In addition to stating behavioral objectives, this book identifies and states the expected criterion for the acceptable level of performance by the student. The criterion is based on 100 percent unless otherwise noted.

An example of a criterion for an objective is as follows: When given a list of common folktale elements, the student will select 75 percent of the elements that are contained in a selected folktale.

The grade level assignments for these objectives are for average students of average achievement. They are not absolutes, since children's levels of understanding and mastery of skills vary considerably even with children of similar ability. These objectives are to be used as guidelines. If previous skills have not been mastered, an expectation that students will learn more complex skills based on unlearned prerequisites is assuring failure for the student. The need to assess the level at which a student is functioning is crucial.

## ASSESSING MASTERY OF PREREQUISITE SKILLS

When students are expected to meet an objective of learning a new task, library media specialists should consider those prerequisite skills that must be a part of the students' repertoire to assure success with the new learning. The classroom teacher and the library media specialist must assess the students' mastery of such prerequisite skills. For example: the library media specialist who asks a student to find definitions in a dictionary within a limited time needs to know whether the student is able to: (1) locate a dictionary, (2) read independently at an appropriate level, (3) alphabetize by the first, second, third, or fourth letter of a word, (4) alphabetize words, and (5) use guide words. That list could go on and on. A student who has a deficiency in any of these prerequisite skills may experience difficulties in learning the new skills. The student may need instruction and experience to learn these prerequisite skills before he or she can be expected to find definitions in a dictionary.

Identification of student learning deficiencies is important for student success. Because a student is gifted or in a high achievement group, the assumption cannot be made that he or she has all the skills needed to accomplish a task.

In reality an instructor does not always have the time that is needed to assess learning deficiencies. Review of needed prerequisite skills, close monitoring of student work, and appropriate intervention when a student has difficulty can minimize the problems that students will encounter. Many students in the third grade and even higher grades do not know the alphabet or how to make use of it. Rather than spend time having students practice the rote learning of the alphabet, the library media specialist may provide students with an alphabet strip (a piece of paper on which the alphabet is printed) and the students can go on with the task and also practice using the alphabet.

The classroom teacher and the library media specialist need to complete a task analysis of what prerequisite skills need to be taught or reviewed in order to assure that the students will be able to meet the subject area curriculum objectives and the library media skills objectives.

## ESTABLISHING INSTRUCTIONAL LIBRARY MEDIA SKILLS OBJECTIVES

The initial process of identifying library media skills objectives for this book led to this outline of four major categories.

I.  Access to Resources
    A.  Staff and Facilities
    B.  Identification and Location of Commercial and Handmade Resources
    C.  Dictionary
    D.  Encyclopedia
    E.  Card Catalog
    F.  Periodicals
    G.  Atlas
    H.  Newspapers
    I.  Almanacs

II.  Selection of Resources

III.  Utilization of Resources
    A.  Use of Print and Nonprint Materials
    B.  Operation of Equipment

IV.  Production of Resources
    A.  Visual Production
    B.  Audio Production
    C.  Audiovisual Production

From the four major categories listed above, the following hierarchy of instructional objectives was developed. An attempt has been made to put objectives into a scope and sequence. This has been done with the understanding that the needs of the student may dictate a rearrangement of the objectives. Some objectives, particularly those that deal with equipment or production, may need to be optional or limited to a smaller percentage of the student population due to budgetary restraints, time limitations, availability of equipment, or philosophy of the local school system or community.

Once an objective is mastered, it may or may not be addressed again. Many objectives need to be maintained and refined. Many skills should be used so that they are not forgotten. Students should use skills in more complex ways as their need for information changes or as they develop related skills (for example, as they use indexes of increasingly sophisticated books). And, of course, for any student who is unable to perform an objective, regardless of grade level, an objective remains an objective.

The following instructional library media skills objectives are written in behavioral terms describing behaviors for children from kindergarten to third grade.

Key:    O   Objective is introduced but not expected to be mastered.
        X   Objective is expected to be mastered by 75% of students.

| | | K | 1 | 2 | 3 |
|---|---|---|---|---|---|
| I. | Access to Resources | | | | |
| A. | Staff and Facilities **The student will:** | | | | |
| 1. | Name personnel of library media center | X | | | |
| 2. | Return materials to appropriate place after use in library media center | O | O | O | O |
| 3. | Request assistance as needed | X | | | |
| 4. | Exhibit behavior that shows consideration for others | O | O | O | O |
| 5. | Tell when library media center is available for use | X | | | |
| 6. | Check out and return materials appropriately according to established procedures: | | | | |
| a. | Books | X | | | |
| b. | Periodicals | X | | | |
| c. | Nonprint materials | X | | | |
| d. | Overnight materials | X | | | |
| e. | Vertical file materials | | | O | X |
| f. | Equipment | | | X | |
| 7. | Relate services that library media staff provide | O | O | O | O |
| 8. | Demonstrate care of print and nonprint materials | O | O | O | O |
| 9. | Demonstrate care of equipment | O | O | O | O |
| 10. | Explain procedure for requesting materials for purchase | O | O | X | |
| B. | Identification and Location of Commercial and Handmade Resources (Print, Nonprint, and Equipment) **The student will:** | | | | |
| 1. | Identify and locate: | | | | |
| a) | Easy collection | X | | | |
| b) | Records | X | | | |
| c) | Record players | X | | | |
| d) | Cassette tapes | X | | | |
| e) | Cassette tape recorders | X | | | |
| f) | Charts (Study prints) | X | | | |
| g) | Picture dictionary | X | | | |
| h) | Filmstrips | X | | | |
| i) | Filmstrip previewers | X | | | |

(Text continues on page 28.)

I. Access to Resources (cont'd)

|  |  | K | 1 | 2 | 3 |
|---|---|---|---|---|---|
| j) | Listening stations and headsets | X |  |  |  |
| k) | Language master cards | X |  |  |  |
| l) | Language masters | X |  |  |  |
| m) | Sound filmstrip previewers | X |  |  |  |
| n) | Film | O | X |  |  |
| o) | 16-mm projector | O | X |  |  |
| p) | Periodicals | O | X |  |  |
| q) | Microcomputer | O | X |  |  |
| r) | Microcomputer program | O | O | O | O |
| s) | Nonfiction collection | O | X |  |  |
| t) | Card catalog | O | O | X |  |
| u) | Dictionaries |  | O | X |  |
| v) | Encyclopedias |  | O | X |  |
| w) | Overhead transparency |  | O | X |  |
| x) | Overhead projector |  | O | X |  |
| y) | Fiction collection |  |  | O | X |
| z) | Vertical file |  |  | O | X |
| aa) | Almanacs |  |  | O | X |
| bb) | Atlases |  |  | O | X |
| cc) | Maps and globes |  |  | O | X |
| dd) | Kits |  |  | O | X |
| ee) | Newspapers |  |  |  | X |
| ff) | Telephone directory |  |  |  | X |
| gg) | Video tape |  |  |  | O |
| hh) | Video tape recorder |  |  |  | O |
| ii) | Opaque projector |  |  |  | O |
| jj) | Realia |  |  |  | O |
| kk) | Slides |  |  |  | O |
| ll) | Slide previewer |  |  |  | O |
| mm) | Slide projector |  |  |  | O |
| nn) | Filmloops |  |  |  | O |
| oo) | Filmloop projectors |  |  |  | O |

2. Identify on print or nonprint material:

|  |  | K | 1 | 2 | 3 |
|---|---|---|---|---|---|
| a) | Cover | X |  |  |  |
| b) | Front | X |  |  |  |
| c) | Spine | O | X |  |  |
| d) | Book pocket | O | X |  |  |
| e) | Book card | O | X |  |  |
| f) | Book jacket | O | X |  |  |
| g) | Title |  | O | X |  |
| h) | Author |  | O | X |  |
| i) | Illustrator |  | O | X |  |
| j) | Call number |  | O | O | X |
| k) | Title page |  | O | O | X |
| l) | Table of contents |  | O | O | X |
| m) | Publisher or producer |  |  | O | X |
| n) | Place of publication |  |  | O | X |
| o) | Copyright or publication date |  |  | O | X |
| p) | Index |  |  | O | X |
| q) | Glossary |  |  |  | O |

I. Access to Resources (cont'd)

| | K | 1 | 2 | 3 |
|---|---|---|---|---|
| r) Appendix(es) | | | | O |
| s) List of illustrations | | | | O |
| t) Map list | | | | O |
| u) Time list | | | | O |
| **3.** Locate a specific book from easy collection when author's last name is known | O | X | | |
| **4.** Explain the arrangement of: | | | | |
| a) Easy collection | O | O | X | |
| b) Fiction collection | | | O | X |
| c) Periodicals | | | O | X |
| d) Nonprint collections | | | O | O |
| e) Vertical file | | | | O |
| f) Reference collection | | | | O |
| g) Special collections | | | | O |
| **5.** Locate by using call numbers: | | | | |
| a) Book from easy collection | O | O | X | |
| b) Fiction book | | | O | O |
| c) Nonfiction | | | O | O |
| d) Nonprint | | | | O |
| **6.** Locate specific information in: | | | | |
| a) Title page | | | O | O |
| b) Table of contents | | | O | O |
| c) Index | | | O | O |
| d) List of illustrations | | | | O |
| e) Map list | | | | O |
| f) Time list | | | | O |
| **7.** Locate information using: | | | | |
| a) Alphabetical order by: | | | | |
| (1) First letter of word | O | O | X | |
| (2) Second letter of word | | | O | X |
| (3) Third letter of word | | | O | X |
| (4) Fourth letter of word | | | | O |
| b) Visuals: | | | | |
| (1) Pictures | O | O | O | O |
| (2) Photographs | O | O | O | O |
| (3) Captions | | | O | O |
| (4) Maps | | | O | O |
| (5) Graphs/Charts | | | O | O |
| (6) Timetable | | | | O |
| c) Dictionary | O | O | O | O |
| d) Title page | | | O | O |
| e) Table of contents | | | O | O |
| f) Guide words | | | O | O |
| g) Index | | | O | O |
| h) Encyclopedia | | | O | O |
| i) Card catalog | | | O | O |
| j) Periodicals | | | O | O |
| k) Newspapers | | | O | O |
| l) Atlas | | | | O |

|  | K | 1 | 2 | 3 |
|---|---|---|---|---|
| **I. Access to Resources (cont'd)** | | | | |
| m) Almanac | | | | O |
| n) List of illustrations | | | | O |
| o) Microcomputer software catalog/menu | | | | O |
| **C. Dictionary** | | | | |
| **The student will:** | | | | |
| 1. Locate information using illustrations in a beginning dictionary | O | O | O | X |
| 2. Locate words in a picture dictionary | | O | X | |
| 3. Locate a specific entry word in: | | | | |
| a) A picture dictionary | | O | X | |
| b) A beginning dictionary | | | O | X |
| c) An intermediate dictionary | | | | O |
| 4. Locate appropriate page for a given entry word using guide words | | | O | X |
| 5. Locate section explaining format of entry in: | | | | |
| a) A beginning dictionary | | | O | X |
| b) An intermediate dictionary | | | | O |
| 6. Locate within an entry in a beginning dictionary: | | | | |
| a) Entry word | | | O | X |
| b) Definition | | | O | X |
| c) Pronunciation | | | O | X |
| d) Syllabication | | | O | X |
| e) Plural spellings | | | O | X |
| f) Part of speech | | | | O |
| 7. Locate correct spelling in a beginning dictionary | | | O | O |
| 8. Identify syllables of an entry word in a beginning dictionary | | | O | O |
| 9. Locate synonym(s) for a given word in a beginning dictionary | | | O | O |
| 10. Locate within an entry in an intermediate dictionary: | | | | |
| a) Entry word | | | | O |
| b) Definition | | | | O |
| c) Pronunciation | | | | O |
| d) Syllabication | | | | O |
| e) Plural spellings | | | | O |
| f) Part of speech | | | | O |
| 11. Locate information using illustrations in an intermediate dictionary | | | | O |
| 12. Locate correct spelling in an intermediate dictionary | | | | O |
| 13. Identify syllables of an entry word in an intermediate dictionary | | | | O |
| 14. Locate synonym(s) for a given word in an intermediate dictionary | | | | O |

| | | K | 1 | 2 | 3 |
|---|---|---|---|---|---|
| I. | Access to Resources (cont'd) | | | | |
| D. | Encyclopedia | | | | |
| | **The student will:** | | | | |
| 1. | Locate the index of an encyclopedia | | | O | X |
| 2. | Locate entry word(s) in the index | | | O | X |
| 3. | Locate specific volume(s) by using letters or numbers on spine | | | O | X |
| 4. | Locate article(s) in a volume by using guide words | | | O | X |
| E. | Card Catalog | | | | |
| | **The student will:** | | | | |
| 1. | Explain the purpose of the card catalog | | | O | X |
| 2. | Find entries by using guide letters and guide words | | | O | X |
| 3. | Identify parts of the catalog card: | | | | |
| | a) Call number | | | O | X |
| | b) Author | | | O | X |
| | c) Title | | | O | X |
| | d) Illustrator | | | O | X |
| | e) Publisher or producer | | | O | O |
| | f) Copyright date | | | O | O |
| 4. | Locate entries by using alphabetizing rules | | | O | O |
| 5. | Identify the media code on catalog card | | | O | O |
| 6. | Identify the three basic types of cards found in the card catalog | | | | O |
| 7. | Locate other sources by using *See* and *See also* | | | | O |
| 8. | Identify subjects related to topic being searched | | | | O |
| 9. | Identify available materials on a specified topic (prepare a list) | | | | O |
| F. | Periodicals | | | | |
| | **The student will:** | | | | |
| 1. | Locate date of publication | | | O | X |
| 2. | Locate table of contents | | | O | X |
| 3. | Locate articles using the table of contents | | | O | X |
| G. | Atlas | | | | |
| | **The student will:** | | | | |
| 1. | Explain the content of an atlas | | | | O |
| 2. | Locate the table of contents of an atlas | | | | O |
| 3. | Locate the index of an atlas | | | | O |
| 4. | Locate the section that provides the key symbols | | | | O |

|  | K | 1 | 2 | 3 |
|---|---|---|---|---|

I.  Access to Resources (cont'd)

|  | K | 1 | 2 | 3 |
|---|---|---|---|---|
| 5. Locate specific location(s) or map(s) in the index | | | | O |
| 6. Locate coordinates and page numbers in the index | | | | O |
| 7. Locate specific map(s) using the index | | | | O |
| 8. Identify special maps (e.g., population and precipitation distribution) | | | | O |

H.  Newspapers

**The student will:**

|  | K | 1 | 2 | 3 |
|---|---|---|---|---|
| 1. Locate masthead | | | | O |
| 2. Locate date of publication | | | | O |
| 3. Name sections of the newspaper | | | | O |
| 4. Locate the index | | | | O |
| 5. Locate specific sections using the index | | | | O |

I.  Almanac

**The student will:**

|  | K | 1 | 2 | 3 |
|---|---|---|---|---|
| 1. Explain the purpose of an almanac | | | | O |
| 2. Explain the content of an almanac | | | | O |
| 3. Explain the frequency of publication | | | | O |
| 4. Locate the index(es) of an almanac | | | | O |
| 5. Locate entry word(s) in the index(es) | | | | O |
| 6. Locate specific article(s) using the index | | | | O |

II. Selection of Resources

**The student will:**

|  | K | 1 | 2 | 3 |
|---|---|---|---|---|
| A. Select materials of interest to student | X | | | |
| B. Select appropriate print materials for student's ability level: | | | | |
|   1. Easy materials | X | | | |
|   2. Nonfiction materials | O | O | O | O |
|   3. Periodicals | O | O | O | O |
|   4. Fiction materials | | | O | O |
| C. Select appropriate nonprint materials for student's ability level | O | O | O | O |
| D. Select appropriate audio equipment for listening: | | | | |
|   1. Record player | X | | | |
|   2. Cassette tape recorder | X | | | |
|   3. Reader/recorder (language master) | O | X | | |
| E. Select a microcomputer program | O | O | O | O |

| | K | 1 | 2 | 3 |
|---|---|---|---|---|
| II. Selection of Resources (cont'd) | | | | |
| F. Select appropriate visual equipment for viewing: | | | | |
| 1. Filmstrip previewer | O | O | X | |
| 2. Filmstrip projector | | | O | O |
| 3. Filmloop projector | | | | O |
| G. Select appropriate audiovisual equipment to use materials that combine audio and visual: | | | | |
| 1. Sound/filmstrip previewer | | O | O | X |
| 2. Sound/filmstrip projector | | | O | O |
| H. Select nonfiction materials for factual information or happenings | | | O | X |
| I. Select dictionary to find: | | | | |
| 1. Word meaning | | | O | O |
| 2. Correct spelling (including plurals) | | | O | O |
| 3. Correct pronunciation | | | O | O |
| 4. Syllabication | | | O | O |
| 5. Parts of speech | | | | O |
| J. Select appropriate part of a print item to locate specific information | | | O | O |
| K. Select an encyclopedia to locate specific information | | | O | O |
| L. Select fiction materials for recount of a made-up occurrence | | | O | O |
| M. Select appropriate resource(s) using card catalog to locate specific information | | | O | O |
| N. Select an overhead projector to show transparency | | | | O |
| O. Select an opaque project to enlarge print material | | | | O |
| P. Select a slide viewer to look at slides | | | | O |
| Q. Select a periodical for current information | | | | O |
| R. Select a newspaper for current information | | | | O |
| S. Select material from the vertical file for information not found in other materials in the library media center | | | | O |
| T. Select a telephone directory to locate needed correct telephone number | | | | O |

| | K | 1 | 2 | 3 |
|---|---|---|---|---|
| **III. Utilization of Resources** | | | | |
| **A. Use of Print and Nonprint Materials** | | | | |
| **The student will:** | | | | |
| 1. Use easy materials for recreational reading/listening | X | | | |
| 2. Use a record for listening | X | | | |
| 3. Use a cassette tape for listening | X | | | |
| 4. Use a picture dictionary | O | X | | |
| 5. Use the cover of a book to find: | | | | |
|    a) Title | O | O | X | |
|    b) Author | O | O | X | |
|    c) Illustrator | | O | O | X |
| 6. Use computer software | O | O | O | O |
| 7. Use visuals to get information | O | O | O | O |
| 8. Use picture clues to decode | O | O | O | O |
| 9. Use audio materials to get information | O | O | O | O |
| 10. Use audiovisual materials to get information | O | O | O | O |
| 11. Use and interpret narrations to: | | | | |
|    a) Predict a character's actions | O | O | O | O |
|    b) Predict the next action | O | O | O | O |
|    c) Predict the ending | O | O | O | O |
|    d) Identify the major sequence of events | O | O | O | O |
|    e) Identify the main idea | O | O | O | O |
|    f) Distinguish between fact and fantasy | O | O | O | O |
|    g) Distinguish between fact and fiction | O | O | O | O |
| 12. Use table of contents to locate information | | O | O | X |
| 13. Use index to locate information | | | O | O |
| 14. Use guide words to locate information | | | O | O |
| 15. Use a dictionary to: | | | | |
|    a) Interpret information within entries by identifying: | | | | |
|       (1) Entry word | | | O | X |
|       (2) Definition | | | O | X |
|       (3) Pronunciation | | | O | O |
|       (4) Plural spellings | | | O | O |
|       (5) Parts of speech | | | | O |
|    b) Select appropriate meaning for a given word | | | O | O |
|    c) Select synonym(s) for a given word | | | | O |
| 16. Interpret maps and globes | | | O | O |
| 17. Interpret simple graphs and charts | | | O | O |
| 18. Identify alternative subject words for topic being investigated | | | | O |
| 19. Use an encyclopedia to locate information by: | | | | |
|    a) Interpreting information in the index to locate specific articles | | | | O |
|    b) Using headings and subheadings | | | | O |

| | K | 1 | 2 | 3 |
|---|---|---|---|---|
| III. Utilization of Resources (cont'd) | | | | |
|     c) Using visuals within an article to get information | | | | O |
|     d) Skimming to find a word/name, phrases, or date | | | | O |
| 20. Paraphrase simple information | | | | O |
| 21. Make a simple outline | | | | O |
| 22. Take simple notes | | | | O |
| 23. Use card catalog to get information by: | | | | |
|     a) Explaining the purpose of the card catalog | | | | O |
|     b) Applying alphabetizing rules | | | | O |
|     c) Using cross-references to determine other related subjects | | | | O |
| 24. Prepare a list of available materials on a specific topic | | | | O |
| 25. Use call number to locate specific materials in library media center | | | | O |
| 26. Use copyright information to determine how current material is | | | | O |
| 27. Use a specific book to locate a specific fact | | | | O |
| 28. Use periodicals to locate information (Students would need assistance in locating information, since they are not expected to know how to use a periodical index. They would be expected to identify on a limited basis which periodicals might be of use. For example: they should know such periodicals as *Ranger Rick* and *National Geographic* might be useful for finding information about animals.) | | | | O |
| 29. Use a simple atlas | | | | O |
| 30. Explain the content of the vertical file | | | | O |
| 31. Use the vertical file to obtain materials | | | | O |
| 32. Use an almanac | | | | O |
| 33. Use a telephone directory | | | | O |
| 34. Use materials in reference collection | | | | O |
| B. Operation of Equipment | | | | |
| **The student will operate correctly and unassisted:** | | | | |
| 1. Record player | X | | | |
| 2. Listening station | X | | | |
| 3. Cassette tape recorder (play and record) | O | O | O | X |
| 4. Filmstrip previewer | O | O | O | X |
| 5. Reader/recorder (language master) | O | O | O | X |
| 6. Sound/filmstrip previewer | O | O | O | X |

| | K | 1 | 2 | 3 |
|---|---|---|---|---|
| III. Utilization of Resources (cont'd) | | | | |
| 7. Microcomputer | | | | |
|   a) Use numbers and letters on keyboard | O | O | O | O |
|   b) Write a simple program | | | O | O |
|   c) Copy a program | | | O | O |
|   d) Save a program | | | O | O |
|   e) Create graphic designs | | | O | O |
| 8. Overhead projector | | O | O | O |
| 9. Opaque projector | | O | O | O |
| 10. Slide previewer | | | O | O |
| 11. Filmstrip projector | | | O | O |
| 12. Instamatic camera | | | O | O |
| 13. Ektagraphic visualmaker | | | | O |
| 14. Slide projector | | | | O |
| 15. 16-mm projector | | | | O |
| 16. Video tape recorder | | | | O |
| 17. Filmloop projector | | | | O |
| IV. Production of Resources | | | | |
| A. Visual Production | | | | |
| **The student will:** | | | | |
| 1. Construct a picture based on ideas from a narrative | O | X | | |
| 2. Illustrate a story by drawing a series of pictures | O | O | O | O |
| 3. Construct a model book including front, back, spine, author, title, publishers, and copyright date | O | O | O | X |
| 4. Mount a picture with school glue | | O | O | X |
| 5. Construct a handmade transparency | | | O | O |
| 6. Construct a machine-made transparency | | | O | O |
| 7. Enlarge a visual using an overhead projector | | | O | X |
| 8. Enlarge a visual using an opaque projector | | | O | X |
| 9. Make a contact print/sun picture | | | O | X |
| 10. Take a picture using an Instamatic camera | | | O | X |
| 11. Create lettering by using a stencil | | | O | O |
| 12. Create lettering by cutting paper | | | O | O |
| 13. Make a handmade slide | | | O | O |
| 14. Make a simple map of the library media center | | | | O |
| 15. Make a handmade filmstrip | | | | O |
| 16. Take a series of pictures with an Instamatic camera | | | | O |
| 17. Take picture(s) using Ektagraphic visualmaker | | | | O |
| 18. Create motion with a series of still pictures (e.g., flip book, animated film) | | | | O |

| | K | 1 | 2 | 3 |
|---|---|---|---|---|
| IV. Production of Resources (cont'd) | | | | |
|    19.  Shoot a Super 8-mm live action film | | | | O |
|    20.  Shoot a Super 8-mm animated film | | | | O |
|   B.  Audio Production | | | | |
|     **The student will:** | | | | |
|    1.  Make a tape recording of own voice | | | O | O |
|    2.  Make a tape recording of live presentation | | | | O |
|    3.  Make a tape recording of prerecorded material | | | | O |
|   C.  Audiovisual Production | | | | |
|     **The student will:** | | | | |
|    1.  Prepare a storyboard | | | O | O |
|    2.  Write script | | | | O |
|    3.  Create visual ideas | | | | O |
|    4.  Select appropriate medium to communicate ideas to intended audience | | | | O |
|    5.  Select appropriate background sound | | | | O |
|    6.  Select appropriate sound effects | | | | O |
|    7.  Produce a slide/tape program | | | | O |
|    8.  Produce a video tape program using one camera | | | | O |

In summary, the foundation of any educational program is the instructional objectives. Instructional objectives must be written in behavioral terms so that student learning behavior can be measured. Instructional objectives must also be developed in a hierarchy. When the classroom teacher and the library media specialist are planning for instruction, they must consider the hierarchy of the instructional objectives. For example: they must consider that the student cannot be expected to locate information in an encyclopedia article until he or she can locate the article.

## BIBLIOGRAPHY

Cupertino Union School District. "K-8 Computer Literacy Curriculum." *The Computing Teacher* 10 (March 1983): 7-10.

Galloway, Charles. *Psychology for Learning and Teaching.* New York: McGraw-Hill, Inc. 1976.

Gillespie, John T., and Diana L. Spirit. *Creating a School Media Program.* New York: R. R. Bowker Company, 1973.

Hart, Thomas. *Instruction in School Media Center Use.* Chicago: American Library Association, 1978.

Prostano, Emanuel T., and Joyce S. Prostano. *The School Library Media Center.* Littleton, Colo.: Libraries Unlimited, Inc., 1971.

Silverman, Eleanor. *101 Media Center Ideas.* Metuchen, N.J.: The Scarecrow Press, Inc., 1980.

Walker, H. Thomas, and Paula Kay Montgomery. *Teaching Library Media Skills.* 2d ed. Littleton, Colo.: Libraries Unlimited, Inc., 1983.

Wehmeyer, Lillian Biermann. *The School Librarian as Educator.* Littleton, Colo.: Libraries Unlimited, Inc., 1976.

# 4 *Identification of Instructional Strategies*

After the decision has been made as to which objectives are to be mastered, the next step is to decide how they will be taught.

## FACTORS FOR CONSIDERATION

Several factors that should be considered are

- the age and developmental level of the students

- the abilities and strengths of the students

- the subject area curriculum

- possible strategies

- materials available

The age and development of the student is a crucial factor. While a third-grade student may be eight years old chronologically; his or her motor, intellectual, physical, and emotional development may be at a much different level. The approach for teaching a group of third-grade students with limited vocabulary development and reading difficulties would be different from the approach used for third-grade students who are reading at or above grade level and have confidence in their ability to learn. Teachers of students who have experienced frustration and failure in the formal learning environment would need to provide work in which the students' success could be assured. They should give these students frequent praise and acknowledgement for their achievement.

As most children develop, they are able to handle more abstract ideas. According to Jean Piaget, preschool and kindergarten students are able to use "symbols to stand for objects, which makes mental manipulation possible." At that age word meanings will be different for different children. The general application of Piaget's theories and findings is that preschool and kindergarten students learn best from *concrete* experiences. The younger the student the more concrete the idea needs to be. That is not to say simply because students are older they can understand abstract ideas. Children in the primary grades (ages six to nine) are eager to learn and have more facility in oral language than in writing. For this age group, the implication from Piaget is that because of intellectual development, students in the primary grades need concrete learning experiences. Additionally, any abstract ideas should be based on concrete understandings. It is essential to start where the students are, not where they should be.[1]

The focus for instruction needs to be placed on the abilities and strengths of the students. If a primary student is able to alphabetize words only with the use of an alphabet strip, the emphasis should be placed on the student's strength (the ability to alphabetize words) rather than on the weakness (needing a crutch to accomplish the task). The attitudes of the student and teacher are very important in the learning situation. If the student and the teacher expect success in the learning environment, they greatly increase the likelihood of success.

Students who learn best through a visual modality would receive maximum benefit from an activity that stressed the visual modality rather than from a lecture type of instruction that relies heavily on the auditory modality. The more senses that are involved in the learning situation, the more likely the student will be successful. While it is not always possible or desirable to involve more than the senses of sound and sight, other senses can be involved in the learning situation. The student who has difficulty learning the alphabet, for example, may benefit from tracing letters made from sandpaper or other textured material as a teacher (or another student or parent or volunteer) says the letter.

The student often needs to be encouraged to be an active learner rather than merely a passive learner. If students are learning about the techniques that Ezra Jack Keats used to illustrate his books, they can certainly view a film about how he created his illustrations. But, in addition, they should be encouraged to try to create similar illustrations. When students are learning about the parts of a book, they can create a book of their own. Learning by doing is always beneficial.

Current philosophy on teaching library media skills focuses on teaching those skills through the subject area curriculum, not in isolation. It makes sense for two reasons: (1) students need a purpose for learning and (2) students can accomplish two or more objectives in one activity. The student who needs to find information to complete a task meaningful to him or her is more motivated to learn. Students who are learning about transportation in social studies can be taught library media skills using transportation as the subject matter. The student who is learning to use an encyclopedia or dictionary by learning about transportation is combining learnings. Within such instruction other areas of curriculum can also be included, such as the arts. Interrelating the arts with academic curriculum is time-effective and enjoyable.

Instructors should consider all the possible strategies for teaching, keeping in mind that the end goal is to teach students how to learn. Some students seem to develop strategies and skills in learning how to learn on their own. Others seem to learn these strategies and skills by accident. These learnings should not be left to incidental instruction but should be considered of primary importance. Eventually, students need to become responsible for their own learning. Students should progress from asking how to obtain books and other materials to coming into a library media center and going directly to the card catalog or other source for locating information. There are many strategies for teaching. Instruction incorporates both a system or order for that instruction and strategies for instruction.

The system for instruction is a plan that ensures that learning takes place. It includes

- objectives
- diagnostic tools and plans
- materials and techniques for learning
- plan for evaluating materials
- plan for evaluating instruction
- criteria for assessment of student learning
- an ongoing reassessment of each part of the system

Without any one of these components of the system, optimal results cannot be expected. The objectives give direction to the library media program. The diagnostic tools and plans can range from informal observation to formal pencil and paper written assessment. Additionally, the diagnosis can and should include information from the classroom teacher or standardized testing. All information gathered is a guide to show the level at which the student is functioning, what is needed to prepare the student to learn the objective, and how the objective can best be met.

Appropriate learning materials and teaching methods need to match the learner and his or her learning style. Methods and materials for instruction can include: lecture, demonstration, informal instruction, use of simulation, gaming, use of learning centers, group discussion, use of every pupil response, use of self-instructional materials, and use of media (films, filmstrips, computers, and so forth). All children do not learn at the same rate and in the same way. The appropriate approach will depend on the students. It is easy to teach in the way that is most comfortable or use materials that are available, but the students should not be expected to fit a mold that is comfortable for the instructor. The instructor should meet the needs of the students. Compromise is sometimes necessary because of such limitations as materials available and time. The students' needs must be the first consideration.

Finally, there needs to be an ongoing reassessment of each part of the total instructional system. Each part of the system is vital to the whole. If any part weakens, the whole system is weakened. A notebook or other record-keeping device should be used to keep track of needed changes or additions.

## GROUPING CONSIDERATIONS FOR INSTRUCTION

Students can be grouped in a variety of ways: homogeneously, heterogeneously, whole class, small interest groups, and reading groups. The type of grouping has implications on the appropriateness of the method of instruction. Limitations of time; space; number of students; scheduling constraints; organizational patterns of the school; and philosophy of the school, community, and school system all impact on the type of groupings possible.

The library media specialist who serves a population of 600 students in an open-space, team-teaching environment may need to provide instruction in an entirely different fashion from that of the library media specialist who serves 350 students in a traditional, individual classroom school. The space and facilities available for instruction will have a bearing on the method of instruction. The school that has a fully equipped television studio added to a library media center will need to make some adjustments from the more traditional approach to teaching library media skills. The time and energy formerly designated to the teaching of the use of the library media center would now need to be expanded to include the teaching of production skills. That is not to suggest that production skills should or could not be taught in a traditional school with limited facilities. The philosophy of the school and the community that has such studio facilities might dictate a different emphasis for instruction. Some areas of the country still have parent volunteers running school libraries, while others have certified library media specialists who in turn have paid library media aides and technical assistants. It is not likely that the majority of students at these two divergent schools would receive the same quality or quantity of instruction. The needs and expectations of such school systems are certainly different. The library media specialist who is shared by two or more schools would probably need to work with larger groups and provide less individualized instruction.

The library media specialist who would like to try a different approach for grouping would need to solicit the support of the principal and/or at least one classroom teacher. Many classroom teachers and principals are reluctant to make any changes. If the school has the traditional scheduling of students in which they are dropped off for library time, a different approach may be desirable. One teacher who is persuaded to allow students to come in small groups or in some other pattern and feels the students have benefited from such a change may generate the news of the benefits for her students.

It is difficult to consider grouping without also considering scheduling. If the library media specialist has classes back-to-back and very little unscheduled time, flexible use of the library media specialist's time is almost impossible. As an objective for one year the library media specialist may want to try to move from totally fixed scheduling to having a portion of each day for flexible scheduling. The support of the administration is important to implementation of this schedule.

Possible grouping considerations are endless. Examples include the following:

1. *Whole class.* Whole classes of primary students can come on a regularly scheduled basis for literature enrichment or library media skills instruction. Then smaller groups from this large group can also come for enrichment, gifted and talented activities, production activities, or skills instruction. There may be specific times when whole class grouping is more desirable than smaller grouping. The beginning of the year for orientation to the library media center and the beginning of a particular unit of study are two such times. An example of combining an appropriate grouping with method of instruction might be when a large number of new books arrive. Demonstrating the method for breaking in a new book and having students break in new books while being instructed is appropriate.

2. *Small interest or ability groups.* Small groups of primary students can come on a regularly scheduled basis for instruction or activities based on an interest, ability, or some other criteria. One group might include students identified as gifted and talented who are scheduled to meet with the library media specialist two or three times a week for an enrichment program that could include doing a novel unit, doing production work, doing research according to their interests, or working on microcomputers. Another group might be able readers who come to the library media center not to meet with the library media specialist, but to continue their participation in a program such as Great Books run by parent volunteers. These small interest or ability groups could change from time to time and would not have to be scheduled regularly. A group of students might come frequently until a task is completed. Another example might be a social studies committee of students who are tasked with researching information and reporting back to the whole class. The library media specialist, as a result of planning with the classroom teacher, may work with such a committee to help guide them through researching their topic, organizing the information into a meaningful format for sharing, and providing needed production skills to create a slide tape or television program. The library media specialist may meet with such a committee three or four times a week on a regular basis for five or six weeks.

3. *Homogeneous grouping.* These groupings may be formed on the basis of reading ability or as a result of assessment for library media skills. Assessments that are developed by the library media specialist or the particular school system can be used. One problem with this type of grouping is the expectation that these students are more similar in learning ability, learning styles, background knowledge, skill development, and speed of task accomplishment than is realistic. Homogeneously grouped students will still have tremendous variations in ability, knowledge, and skills. These factors should be kept in mind when planning and working with homogeneously grouped students.

4. *Heterogeneous grouping.* Heterogeneous groupings of classes may be determined by school or community philosophy. These groups, whether whole classes or small groups, may be formed for a variety of reasons. For example: If a whole class is working on a unit in social studies, the classroom teacher may want to create committees for investigations with students of mixed abilities. The purpose of such groupings may be to create an atmosphere where cooperation and other social skills are practiced, as well as to provide a situation where less able students will learn from and be assisted by more able students. One or more of such social studies groups may come to the library media center for

instruction as a result of joint planning between the library media specialist and the classroom teacher. One group may come because their assignment requires that they be introduced to the use of an almanac; another may need assistance in locating easy-to-read or audiovisual materials on their topic; and another group may need to learn how to plan and write a script, how to use a 35-mm camera, and how to make a sound track for a slide/tape production.

There are many possible ways of grouping students for library media skills instruction. While there are many factors that impact on the use of the possible instructional groupings, the primary reason for grouping would be to meet the needs of the students.

## REWARDING STUDENT ACHIEVEMENTS AND ACCOMPLISHMENTS

Human beings need rewards for achievements and accomplishments. Adults can be heard making comments such as, "I know I didn't do a bad job on that task or she would have yelled," or "It would have been nice to get some recognition that I did a good job—anything, a letter, a you-did-a-good job comment—it would have meant so much." These comments reflect the need for recognition and approval. Children have the same need for recognition and approval.

Such recognition for achievements and accomplishments can range from a smile or gentle touch to certificates. If slips are used to monitor progress, the initialing of a completed task is recognition. (See chapter 6, "Evalutation, Assessment, and Record Keeping," for an example.) The library media specialist may want to create a special certificate to recognize accomplishments. A Happy Gram award (fig. 4.1) could be designed and given to each student when a task is learned or a center is finished.

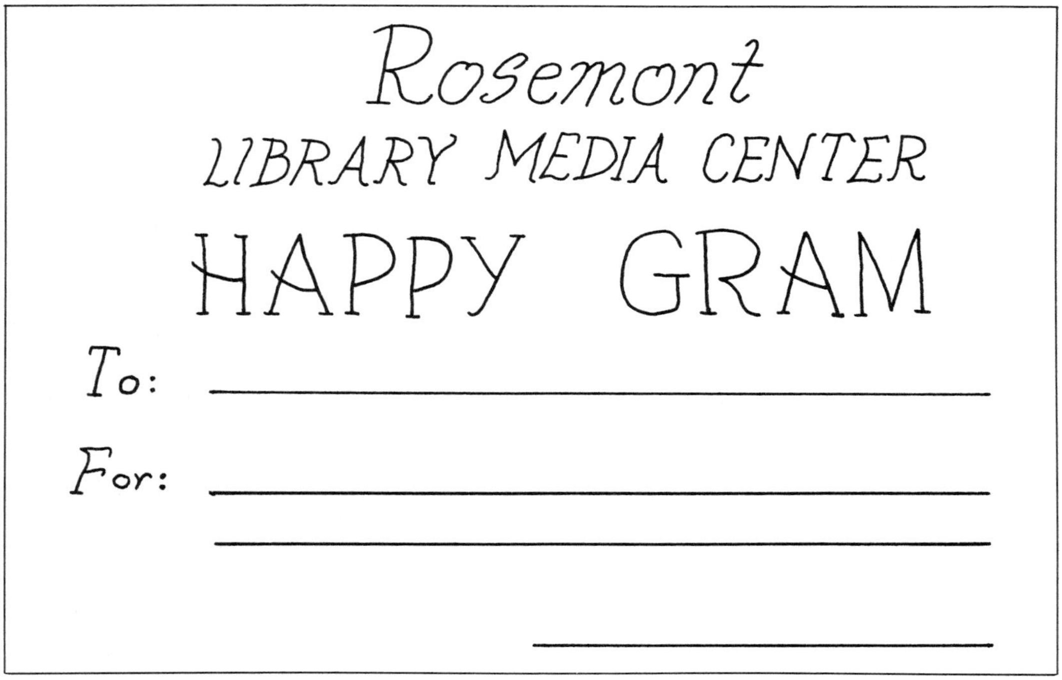

Fig. 4.1. Happy Gram award.

The Happy Gram could be designed by students, the library media specialist, or a graphic artist. If the school has a Happy Gram, it could be used to support the idea that skills learned in the library media center are part of the total school program. A more elaborate Library Media Center Award (fig. 4.2) could be given for major accomplishments.

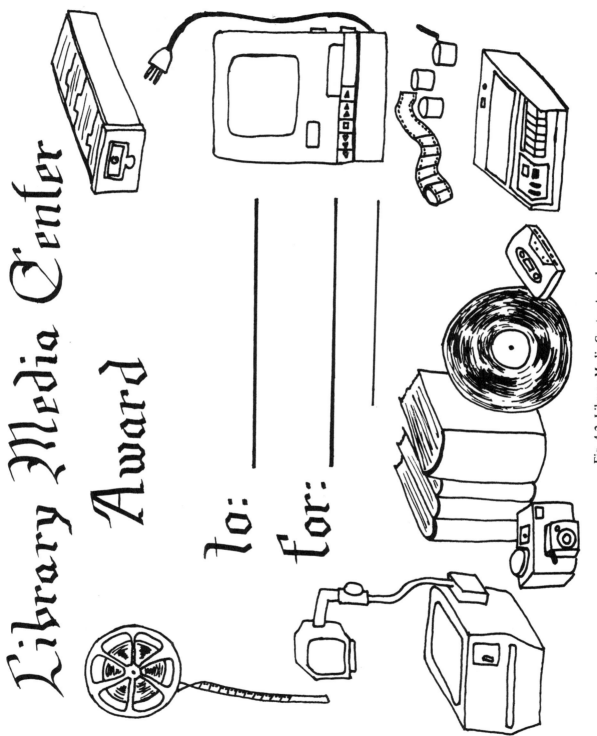

Library Media Center Award

to: _____

for: _____

Fig. 4.2. Library Media Center Award.

An accomplishment chart (fig. 4.3) could be made on heavy board for display in the classroom. When a student finishes a center or completes a task, his or her name could be added noting the accomplishment and the date.

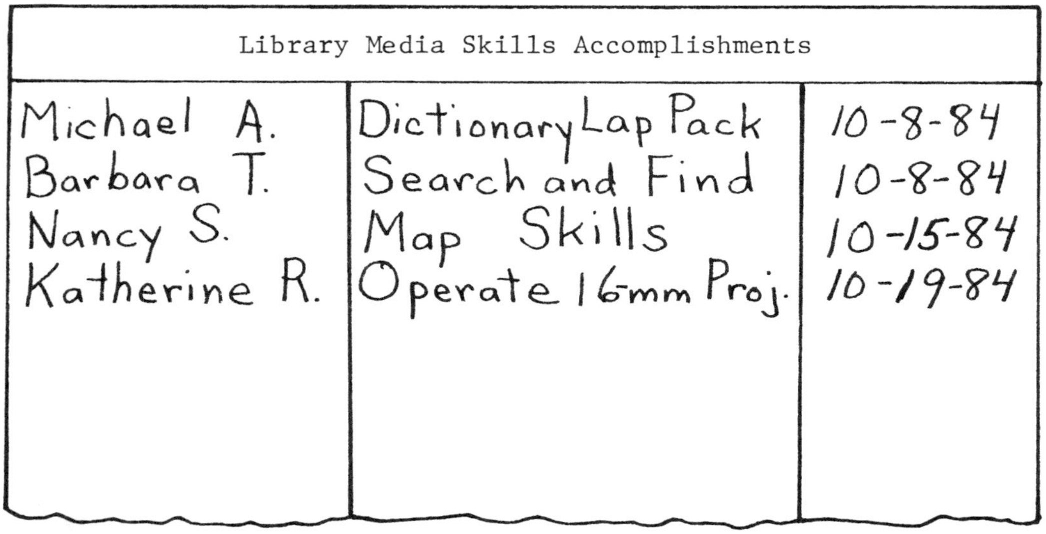

| Library Media Skills Accomplishments | | |
|---|---|---|
| Michael A. | Dictionary Lap Pack | 10-8-84 |
| Barbara T. | Search and Find | 10-8-84 |
| Nancy S. | Map Skills | 10-15-84 |
| Katherine R. | Operate 16mm Proj. | 10-19-84 |

Fig. 4.3. Library Media Skills Accomplishments chart.

These recognitions that are given to the student not only encourage the child to repeat achieving behavior but also create good public relations between the school and home. Children look forward to taking their Happy Gram home or back to their classroom teachers. The library media specialist who combines a positive attitude with deserved praise can help create an atmosphere where learning is encouraged, accomplished, and enjoyed.

## METHODS AND MATERIALS

A variety of methods and materials will be presented. No method or material is a panacea. Some methods or materials may not be appropriate for the primary student. Other approaches may be appropriate for some students but not for others or appropriate in one situation but not in another. Each method or material has advantages and disadvantages. The advantages have to be weighed against the disadvantages.

### Lectures

The lecture method largely relies on information being transmitted to students verbally, and it is not generally an appropriate method of instruction for primary students. Young students need to have visual and auditory stimulation for instruction because of their developmental level. The primary student needs concrete instruction. Lecture may be combined with demonstration to be effective. If, for example, young children are *told* where to place unwanted materials when they are finished with them, they also need to be *shown* where to place materials. Young students may not have enough facility with language to comprehend what they are being told. Or, they may think they understand, but do not.

## Demonstrations

Demonstrations are appropriate methods for the initial understanding of a concept or technique, of a library media center tool, or of equipment. In a demonstration, the instructor shows or simulates a technique, process, or procedure. The danger occurs if the instruction is limited to this method or stops at this point. Students need to have actual experiences. They need to use the actual projector, index, almanac, or encyclopedia. In other words, practice must follow demonstration. The overhead projector can be a valuable tool for doing demonstrations for large groups of students. While it is ideal to work with individuals or small groups, school restraints beyond the library media specialist or the principal's control may prohibit such instructional grouping.

When preparing for a demonstration, the library media specialist needs to walk through the activity mentally to see that the activity matches the objective and that the activity flows smoothly. This mental check will assure that all needed materials and equipment are available. The steps of the demonstration can be written in an outline on an index card to help prevent part of the lesson from being left out. This outline should be in plain sight for easy referral when doing a demonstration. This technique should be organized to follow the format of other instruction lessons: stated objective(s), grade level, materials and/or equipment needed, procedure, and assessment.

### *SAMPLE DEMONSTRATION*

OBJECTIVES:

The student will be able to fill out check out card, place the card in the appropriate box, and put a due date slip in the pocket of the book.

GRADE LEVEL: First

MATERIALS/EQUIPMENT NEEDED:

Books of students' choice

Pencils

Overhead projector

Screen

Transparency of sample book card (fig. 4.4, see page 38)

Pencil/Pen to write on transparency

Assistants to check on students' cards as they are filling them out

PROCEDURE:

At the beginning of the school year, first-grade students need to learn how to fill out the library book card. After the students have chosen their book, they can be seated facing the screen. Make sure that all students have a pencil. Explain that the students are going to fill out their own library book card. Have students locate and remove the book card from the book pocket. Turn on the projector and tell the students that the card on the screen is just like the one they have. Show the students that the first column is for placement of the due date. Then show them where they can locate the due date when they check out books. Have a student tell what the due date is that day. Write the due date on the transparency. Show and tell them that they are to write on the first blank line. Then, have students write the due date on their own card. It may be necessary to show students how to write some of the numbers. The edges of the transparency can be used to demonstrate how to write numbers. While they are writing the due date, the library media specialist and any

| E S | | 200 |
|---|---|---|
| Sendak<br>Chicken soup with rice | | |

| DATE DUE | BORROWER'S NAME | ROOM NO. |
|---|---|---|
| 9-15 | Robin S. | 7 |
| 9-18 | Jonathan N. | 10 |
| | | |
| | | |
| | | |
| | | |
| | | |
| | | |
| | | |
| | | |
| | | |
| | | |
| | | |
| | | |

**Fig. 4.4. Sample book card for overhead transparency.**

assistants can check that the students are doing it correctly. If a student has difficulty locating the first blank line, a small dot can be placed on that line and student instructed to write on the line that has the dot. When the students have that part correct, tell students that they are to put their first name and last initial on the next column. Ask several students what they are going to put on their book card. Then have a student who might have difficulty tell what they should write. Write that student's name on the transparency. While they are writing their names, the library media specialist and assistants should check that they are doing it correctly. When the students have completed that task, tell them that they are to write their room number in the last column. Ask if anyone knows what their room number is. If they do, write the room number on the transparency.

If they don't, tell them and write the number on the transparency. Tell them that as soon as they are finished writing their room number, they are to line up at the desk, let you check their card, put it in the box for cards, and take a blue due date card to put in the pocket of their book—not their pants pocket. After students have done this, instruct them to sit down and look at their book.

ASSESSMENT:

Were the students able to fill out the card, deposit it in the appropriate box, and put a due date slip in the book pocket? Students are to be assisted until they are able to accomplish this activity (unless there is some difficulty, such as speaking another language or not knowing how to write their numbers or name). It is expected that this lesson will be repeated; the students will not be expected to check out a book unassisted the next time.

When doing a demonstration, the use of audiovisual equipment and materials can be beneficial, because they can provide information that might otherwise be unclear. An overhead transparency, for example, with overlays of a sample catalog card would be useful to demonstrate how to interpret the given information and understand the layout of the catalog card. Once this has been done, students need to have the actual experience of interpreting information on a card in the catalog. A film or filmstrip showing how to locate information in an encyclopedia can provide organization to instruction as well as visuals that are large enough for the students to see clearly. One thought should be kept in mind when using audiovisual materials: the entire material does not have to be used. Additionally, a film can be stopped to clarify a concept or point out an inaccuracy or practice that does not apply to the particular school. Just because a film is fifteen minutes long does not mean the students have to view the entire film. A combination of verbal instructions, use of part of a film or filmstrip, and actual hands-on experience may be preferable.

Students can be involved in this activity by (1) answering questions, (2) actually writing on the overhead, (3) pointing to a place or part (if using a transparency of a catalog card, students might point to some part of the card), and (4) asking questions.

**Informal Instruction**

Informal instruction can range from the appropriate use of terminology when talking to students to providing a model when helping a student find a book. For example: when using a filmstrip, tell the students that they will be viewing a *filmstrip*. Young students often call a filmstrip a *film*. When introducing a book during story time for kindergarten and first-grade students, the library media specialist can informally teach the parts of a book. If the story time centers around an author, the library media specialist can tell how the call number on an easy book is composed and show them where other books by that author can be located.

Another time that informal instruction can be used is when students come to the library media center for books on a certain topic. Rather than showing or telling very young students where the dinosaur books are located, the library media specialist can provide a model for the students, showing them how to use the card catalog to locate such books. This provides a behavior model for the students to follow when they attain the needed skills. Most library media specialists could show or tell a student where books are to be found on dinosaurs, football, or other popular topics with little difficulty; however, valuable informal instruction might be lost.

The library media specialist could take the students through the entire process of finding a book. This could be done by first noting the outside guides on the drawers of the card catalog. The library media specialist could find the *D* drawer and say, "Dinosaurs would be in this *D* drawer." Then he or she could say the call number while writing it on scrap paper. Using that written call number to locate a specific book on the shelves would contribute to learning informally that the card catalog is a useful tool to locate needed books or materials that are housed in the library media center.[2]

When a student comes into the library media center for some material, the student may or may not ask for assistance. A process of checking what the student wants (reference questioning) often provides a good time for informal instruction. The young student often has difficulty expressing what is needed and may not have a clear understanding of what is needed to accomplish an assignment. For example: A second-grade boy comes into the library media center and requests assistance in locating a book or other material on dogs. After asking the student why he wants the material, the library media specialist may find that the student is getting a puppy and wants information on taking care of a puppy. The student does not want a book on different kinds of dogs but a book on the care and training of a puppy. The questioning process may help the student to be more precise in telling what he wants on another occasion. The library media specialist who is alert to a student's questions and body language will use each informal opportunity to guide a student in locating and using library media center materials and equipment.

Here is another example. A young girl who comes into the library media center, wanders around, and does not ask for assistance may be exhibiting body language that indicates a teachable moment has arrived. The way she seems to be searching for something rather than wasting time and the puzzled look on her face suggest she needs assistance. This informal teachable moment might have been lost if the library media specialist had not read the girl's body language.

The number of opportunities to teach young students informally is endless. This can be accomplished through a conscientious effort to discover new ways of teaching informally and to look at some current practices that might be modified.

## Gaming

Games as educational tools came into widespread use in the early 1960s. Games used for instruction should be used with specific objectives for learning in mind. The library media specialist needs to determine whether the objective will be met by using a game and whether the game is the most appropriate learning method to accomplish the objective. Use of games requires the instructor to plan for their use as he or she would for any other instructional activity.[3] The library media specialist needs to evaluate any game prior to and during student use to assure that the objectives are being met. He or she needs to determine whether a game actually teaches what it is supposed to teach.[4]

There are advantages to using games.

1. A wide range of achievement levels can be met by using games.[5]

2. Games are useful in the important step of motivating the learner toward a goal.

3. Development of positive attitudes toward a particular subject area can be accomplished through the use of games.[6]

4. The learning environment and teacher/student relationships may be improved through the use of games.

5. Instructors and students can develop their own games. These games do need to meet specific student needs and objectives.[7]

There are limitations to using games.

1. The time needed to play games is often out of proportion to the amount of learning that takes place.

2. Some students will not accomplish the expected objective of the game.

3. Some students may become more involved with the mechanics of the game (i.e., moving the pieces on a gameboard) and lose sight of the game's instructional objective.

A game that could be used with first-grade students might be one where they could become detectives to help an easy book find where its "home" is located. They could be given an easy book that needs to be put away. When they find their book's home, they could raise their hand for the library media specialist to check that they have located the correct address.

Second graders could participate in a treasure hunt to locate specific materials in the library media center. Students could be teamed and given slips of paper on which the items they are to locate are listed. After the library media specialist verifies their "treasure," each member can be given a bookmark or similar treasure.

## Learning Center Approach

A learning center is a self-paced, self-contained package of learning activities that have a planned progression. The learning center can be diagnostic, instructional, or a combination of the two. In an instructional mode, the learning center can be introductory or a reinforcement of library media skills. Ideally, learning centers should use subject area curriculum as the vehicle for library media skills instruction or diagnosis. Learning centers can provide students with the opportunity to be responsible for their own learning and to work at their own rate. One argument for homogeneous grouping with the learning center approach is that the students are more similar on one or more characteristics important to learning than when grouped heterogeneously. The reality is that there are still many variations in learning style, rate, motivation, and previous experience among homogeneously grouped students. Using learning centers can provide for some of these differences.

There are several advantages to using learning centers. Students can be responsible for their own learning. Students can work at their own pace. Learning centers provide for individual differences of students. Learning centers are easy to store, and learning centers do not generally need constant revision.

The library media specialist who wants to move toward a learning center approach for formal instruction must plan ahead. It takes time to implement such an approach and to create such learning materials. It may seem that the first center takes forever before it is useful. But, as one gains some experience, making learning centers becomes easier and takes less time. Setting a goal of making two or three the first year or perhaps one a month would be reasonable. Once a learning center is made, it is done; when revisions are needed, they can be done quickly. Sometimes other library media specialists have a similar interest in this approach and sharing and trading finished products can be considered.

The first step toward a learning center approach is to determine what needs to be added to what is presently available for instruction. Then a learning center can be made on that topic or type of material. For example: If a need exists to have additional materials to teach third-grade students the use of the dictionary, that may be the place to begin. If focusing on a particular author or social studies topic for second-grade students is a high priority, that might be the place to start. If the school is implementing a new social studies curriculum, part of that could be integrated with particular library media skills. If the principal informs the staff that the school is receiving a microcomputer, a learning center for students and staff to learn some basic skills needed to operate it might be appropriate.

The learning center should have six parts: (1) a title, (2) stated purpose(s) or objective(s), (3) clear, simple directions, (4) adequate instructions, (5) appropriate activities, and (6) an evaluation of learning. Additionally, the learning center needs to be attractive, easy to store, durable, and not in need of constant replenishment of materials.

The same steps and considerations used in producing instructional materials apply when creating learning centers. One must (1) decide on objectives, (2) brainstorm ideas, (3) gather materials and resources, (4) evaluate what is available, (5) allow thinking time, (6) outline activities, (7) make activities, (8) plan layout, (9) do graphics, (10) test learning center with students, (11) revise learning center if needed, (12) make it durable, and (13) continually reassess the learning center.

Learning centers can take many forms. They can be made into bulletin boards, freestanding units, or single boards that can be posted. Where and how the learning center is to be used, the number of students using it, and storage considerations when not in use will be factors in deciding what form the learning center should take.

The freestanding unit (fig. 4.5) that can have two or more panels is a model that is easy to store and retrieve.

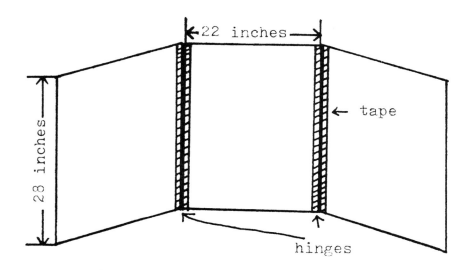

**Fig. 4.5. Suggested model for freestanding learning center.**

A smaller version (fig. 4.6) is the table-sized learning center.

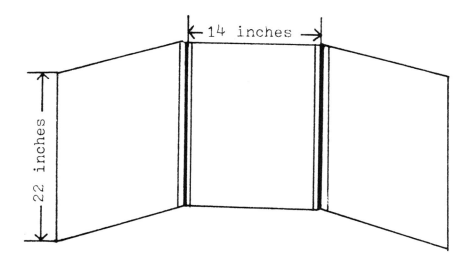

**Fig. 4.6. Suggested model for table-sized learning center.**

This type of center can be self-contained. Pockets can be attached to hold such materials as activity sheets, maps, periodicals, and pamphlets. If a cassette needs to be attached to the learning center, two holes need to be drilled in the top of the back of the cassette case (fig. 4.7). Then, matching holes need to be put through the center's panel. Thin, plastic coated wire or similar material can be used to attach the case to the center.

Fig. 4.7. Cassette case with drilled holes.

When four or more panels are put together, they can be placed on a table in a circular pattern (fig. 4.8) or zigzagged back and forth (fig. 4.9) so that several students could use the center at one time.

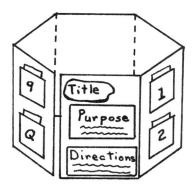

Fig. 4.8. Learning center placed in a circular pattern.

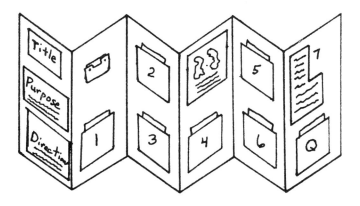

Fig. 4.9. Learning center placed in a zigzag pattern.

There are a number of ways to evaluate student work. Students can check their own work if answers are provided at the learning center. This method does not always work well if questions or tasks are open-ended. This barrier can be eliminated if the evaluation is done by the library media specialist or the library media specialist and the student. Both the library media specialist and the student need to be involved at some point.

An easy method for keeping answer sheets readily available is stapling answer sheets to the inside of file folders and labeling the file folders with the title of the learning centers for which the answers apply. Then the file folders can be put in a Princeton file or similar container for quick reference. This method or a similar method is necessary if students are involved in many different activities at one time.

*Planning Layout*

At this point consideration needs to be given to how the finished learning center will look. How can this center be made easy for the students to use and follow? How and what sources can be used to make this center appealing and attractive?

The number of panels and size of the panels are determined by who this is for: one student, a small group of students, or a whole class. If it is to be used by one student at a time, a small mini-center that can be placed in front of the student on a desk or table might be made. If it is for a small group of students or a whole class, a learning center that can be freestanding and placed on the floor might be useful. If there are only four or five activities, they may fit on a center with three panels. Depending on the size and number of the activities, more than three panels may need to be made. This can be determined when the layout is done. It may be desirable to make a learning center for use on a bulletin board. This format does pose some problems: it is not easily accessible to students when it is not on display; it may be difficult to store when not in use; or it may tie up a large area for a limited number of students. In spite of these difficulties, it does offer another format. A learning center in bulletin board format may be useful for timely activities such as orientation to the library media center at the beginning of the school year, or for a special topic that would be appropriate or of interest to most students such as black history or contributions by women.

The learning center should be easy for the student to use and follow. One of the most important ways in which this can be accomplished is by the use of simple, clear language. Arrows, numbers, and/or clear instructions to direct students from one activity to another can also be useful.

If a freestanding unit is being made, the panels of the center should be sturdy yet be capable of being cut. Mounting board seems to be relatively durable. A good grade of three-inch thick, heavy-duty bookbinding tape is needed to attach the panels. To attach two panels, lay them face down on a flat surface about one-quarter inch apart. At first, two people may be needed to attach the tape. Taping should be started at the top of the panels going down to the bottom. The tape should not be cut. Then the panels should be turned right side up. (This step is a little tricky.) The tape should be brought up over the bottom edge and all the way to the top of the panels. Now the tape can be cut about three inches above the top of the panels. The extra three-inch piece should be brought over the top and placed down on the back. Running the fingers over the section where the two panels are connected will create a hinge. If more than three panels are needed, it is easier to do sets of two panels and then assemble those rather than adding one panel at a time.

*Organizing Students' Work*

Since students will be unable to finish most centers in one session, a plan is needed for organizing students' papers so valuable time will not be lost. One method that seems to work well is to use either a Princeton file or box to hold the file folders that contain the students' work (see fig. 4.10). On the outside of each folder, the following information should be put in pencil: (1) the teacher's name, (2) the day and time students come to the library media center, and (3) the students' names. The reason for putting this information in pencil is that such information frequently changes. These folders can be organized by the order in which classes or groups come to the library media center. In this folder, students' work can be stapled to slips used to monitor progress of individual activities. Each student's progress card can also be kept in this file folder. See chapter 6, "Evaluation, Assessment, and Record Keeping," for more information on these record-keeping devices. As students come into the library media center, they can retrieve their work from their folder and resume the task immediately.

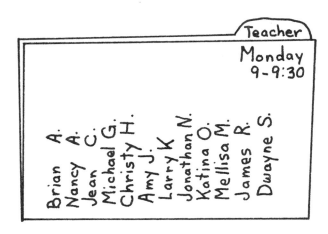

**Fig. 4.10. Group file folder for students' work.**

*Checking Students' Work*

Students can come to have their work checked after every question, at the end of an activity, at the end of a short center, or in any variation that seems appropriate. Within the same group of students who are working on the same task, some students may need their work checked after each answer, others after two or three answers, while yet others may complete an entire activity before having their answers checked. Knowing and monitoring the students will provide valuable information as to which approach is appropriate for each student. Some students seem to know when they are on the wrong track, while others seem to have no idea. The latter student would definitely need to be checked more often. Students who have difficulty and do not easily ask for assistance may need to be told to come to have answers checked after a specified time period—five or ten minutes. Even if the required work is not written work, an assessment of how and what the student is doing to accomplish the task can be done. For example: Assistance can be given to a student who is having difficulty finding entry words in a dictionary. The library media specialist should observe the students for any signs that they are having difficulties. A little intervention or direction here can save the students valuable time, prevent misunderstandings, and keep the students on task.

When checking a student's work, an attempt should be made to find out how or why the student came to an incorrect answer. Since many people learn more from their mistakes, it is important to have students understand their mistakes and be able to arrive at a correct or appropriate answer. There is little point in having students do a task, if they are not expected to accomplish it. Students soon learn what is expected or accepted. Wrong answers should not be accepted. If students are expected to be able to use captions to gain information in an encyclopedia, then incorrect answers should not be accepted. Telling the student an answer or how to get an answer may not be as useful to the student as guiding him or her into such a discovery. One of the tasks of library media specialists should be to help students learn how to learn.

## Group Discussion

Group discussion occurs when either the instructor or the student poses a question or problem and members of the group attempt to answer the question or solve the problem. Group discussion can range from informal, where rules do not exist beyond the expectancy of respectful behavior, to the purposefully structured formal discussion that has guidelines. Great Books discussion groups are for students from grade two through post-graduate levels. In Great Books discussions, each person has read the same selection, one that is generally considered a classic piece of literature. The leaders pose open-ended questions that pertain to the selection. Information from other sources cannot be used in the discussion, since all members of the group may not have read it. Participants are called to support their answers by proof from the selection. In a democratic discussion, each member has an equal voice to have his or her opinion heard. Group members may request that the individual who has given an opinion or alleged fact support his or her contribution to the discussion with some supporting evidence. Students need to be able to explain their task, which is to be accomplished during the discussion group. They need a clear understanding of what they are discussing and how or what they are to do with their conclusions.

### Guidelines for Discussion

Each member's point of view should be respected, but it can be challenged for supporting information. Each member has the right to present his or her point of view. Each member should be encouraged to participate. Members should not be allowed to monopolize the discussion.

This technique of having students contribute information can be useful. An example of an effective use of group discussion would be when students are starting a unit of study on Eskimos. Students can be divided into groups to decide what they want to find out about Eskimos. Prior to having students do a slide tape project where they need to use a number of resources for gaining information, the library media specialist may have students discuss what resources would be useful to obtain information. This last activity could be, in part, an informal assessment.

Another example of an effective use of this method for primary students is in the area of comprehending literature. After reading or listening to a selection, students could discuss such open-ended questions as: (1) why a character behaved the way he or she did, (2) what the problem and solution were in the selection, and (3) what elements of folktales were present in a particular folktale. Students might be put into small discussion groups and given the same or a different question. After a given time, students could be brought back together to relate their findings.

### Drawbacks of This Method

There are several drawbacks to the group discussion of instruction for primary students. The time spent on this type of instructional technique may not be the most efficient in terms of amount of learning accomplished. In addition, students who do not have prerequisite skills and/or knowledge may not gain new knowledge as a result of listening to others talk. Primary students may not be able to contribute as much as older students because of their lack of experience and knowledge.

## Every Pupil Response

Every pupil response is a technique in which all students respond to the teacher's question by some nonverbal communication. Several ways of responding can be used. If answers are of a Yes or No nature, students can use one hand to indicate their response. Their hand straight up and down near their chin can mean Yes (fig. 4.11) and crossways at their chin can mean No (fig. 4.12).

Fig. 4.11. Student showing nonverbal response of Yes.

Fig. 4.12. Student showing nonverbal response of No.

By keeping the response close to the face, a student would not be as able to see other students' answers. After students have given their response, the library media specialist can give the same type of response indicating the correct answer. Another way would be to give students index cards that contain possible answers. The library media specialist can cue students when to show their response. Again, after students have displayed their answer, the library media specialist can show students the correct answer.

When teachers use questioning as a method to teach and evaluate, often only a handful of students participate. One reason is that only one student can verbally respond at one time and be understood. Additionally, there is a tendency for the self-assured, more able student to volunteer and be verbal; while others tend to try to go unnoticed and remain quiet. This type of behavior can be modified by changes in the environment and awareness of some questioning techniques. The every pupil response method allows all students to respond to questioning. The library media specialist can also visually assess instantly what is being understood and give immediate feedback to the students.

An example of an appropriate use of this method would be when third-grade students are learning what reference tool is most appropriate to find a specific answer. Students can be given a set of cards that are labeled, for example, index, dictionary, atlas, telephone book (fig. 4.13). Review and teaching the sight recognition of these words may be necessary. Then the library media specialist can pose such questions to the students as: What is the best source to use to find a map of Mexico? What is the best source to use to find the telephone number for the police? What is the best source to use to find the definition of "export?"

**Fig. 4.13. Student showing response with labelled card.**

Another example of an appropriate use of this method would be after second-grade students have been taught the motifs of folktales. Every pupil response could be used to assess whether students were able to recognize which motifs of folktales were found in a selection they had just heard. As the various motifs of folktales are named, students could respond Yes or No about the use of that particular motif in that folktale. If a student responds in a manner that seems inappropriate, the student can be asked to give the reason and support for his or her response. If his or her reasoning is plausible, the student's answer could then be accepted. This nonverbal approach is a pleasant change, involves more students, and gives more immediate feedback to responses than many more traditional questioning methods.

## Task Cards

Task cards can be produced that are self-paced and self-instructional. A set of task cards can contain a single activity or multiple activities. Usually each task card contains one concept and each activity builds on skills developed on previous cards. Standardization of size is particularly useful when considering storage. Activities can be mounted on railroad board that has been cut to such standardized sizes as 6" x 8" or 8½" x 11". These task cards can then be stored in boxes, file folders, portfolios, or manila envelopes. A shipping box that contained a cassette recorder or examination copies of textbooks can be used to store a set of activity cards. The box can be covered and labeled with title, purpose, and directions. Drawings, pictures, and other graphics can be added to make the box attractive.

One example of a possible set of task cards might be for use of a microcomputer. Task card one: Student learns to turn on and off the computer. Task card two: Student learns to use the keyboard. Task card three: Student learns how to load commercial program. Task card four: Student learns how to run commercial program. Task card five: Student learns how to write own program. Task card six: Student learns how to list own program. Task card seven: Student learns how to run own program. Task card eight: Student learns how to save own program. Task card nine: Student learns how to verify own program.

Instructional materials need to be attractive, but the display of learning materials must also be attractive and functional. After task cards are laminated, they can be displayed in several ways. Two wide styrofoam cups with slots cut out of the bottom can be set upside down to accommodate a single, lightweight task card (figures 4.14 and 4.15, see page 50).

**Fig. 4.14. Cut styrofoam cup used for task card display.**

**Fig. 4.15. Task card displayed on two styrofoam cups.**

Two stands for heavier cards can be made from corrugated box that has been cut and then covered with an attractive adhesive paper (fig. 4.16). First, the top and bottom of the corrugated box should be removed. Then the sides should be cut at opposite corner folds. Cut a lightening bolt zigzag. When opened up, it will hold an instructional card. In figure 4.17 a student is working on a task card that is being held by a corrugated box stand.

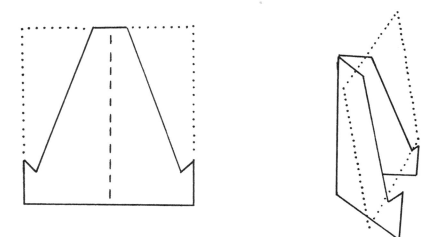

**Fig. 4.16. Stand for heavy task cards.**

Fig. 4.17. Student working on a task card. Task card is held by a corrugated box stand.

### Booklets or Lap Packs

Booklets or lap packs are forms of self-paced, programmed, or organized learning instructional materials. These are intended to be used independently and at the student's own pace. These can be used as follow-up to instruction, review of skills previously learned, actual learning materials that contain instruction, or some combination. They can be made so that students can write their responses directly in the booklet or on separate paper. For very young students or for students who have difficulty transferring information from one place to another, it is preferable that they write directly in the booklet. The older student or more able student can write on a separate sheet of paper, eliminating the need to replenish the material for other students. As with other learning materials, booklets or lap packs need to be attractive; meet the objectives to be learned; have simple, clear directions; be appropriate for the age, abilities, and/or interests of the student; be efficient in terms of time spent on task compared to amount of learning; and durable (if they are to be used by more than one student). If the booklet is to be used by more than one student, additional copies may be made on a quality copy machine. Such a machine may be available for use at some central location within the school system. If the students are expected to write in the booklet and multiple copies have been made using a ditto master, the library media specialist needs to make sure the copies are clear and easy to read. If possible, it is desirable to coordinate other subject area curricula with library media skills objectives. Booklets can be self-checking or checked by the library media specialist and the student. (See chapter 8 for model activity "Animal Dictionary Lap Pack.")

To make the booklets more durable, the pages can be assembled like a book. If acetate sheets are available, they can be used as outside covers. If a laminating machine is accessible, laminating the title and back page make the booklet much more durable. After laminating or putting acetate sheets on the front and back, the booklet should be stapled together using a heavy-duty stapler if necessary.

Booklets or lap packs can be made for the primary student on the use of the alphabet, picture dictionary, pre-encyclopedia, and encyclopedia. This type of instruction allows students to work at their own pace. Since many young students enjoy taking booklets home, this format of instructional materials appeals to many primary students.

### Student-made Models

Young students can create actual models of some tools in the library media center. When such models are created, they can become part of the library media center collection. The student who actually makes or helps make a picture dictionary, book, or slide tape production will have a better understanding of that medium than if he or she were merely shown an example. A class of beginning readers could make a picture dictionary in which they illustrate words they are learning to read. Not only would this help students learn new words, but it would also help them gain an understanding of the concept of a dictionary.

Young students can learn the parts of a book by creating a class, group, or individual book. By including a cover, title page, dedication, and text, students are gaining a clearer understanding of the parts of a book than if they are merely shown the parts. One activity that is fun, educational, and good for public relations is creating a book for the classroom teacher based on Mercer Mayer's book entitled *Just for You.* The activity is given in chapter 8.

Another activity that is useful for the understanding of an important tool of the library media center is having young students prepare a class card catalog. Students can make individual, simplified author cards for a favorite easy book. This activity can be continued when students find other books they would like to add. After students have gained an understanding of the organization of the easy collection, the library media specialist may want to continue this activity to include favorite books from the nonfiction section. Creating a card catalog needs to be combined with locating books by using the class card catalog. (See the model activity "Student-made Card Catalog" in chapter 8.)

### Media

The use of various media such as films, filmstrips, and computer programs has long been lauded. These media provide a great assistance in the instruction of students. Media can be used most effectively when a few simple guidelines are followed.

1. All materials should be previewed prior to use with students.

2. The library media specialist must be responsible for planning for the use of the media. The lesson using media needs to have stated objectives, a definite procedure for use, and assessment.

3. A purpose for viewing and using the medium must be stated to the students.

4. Follow-up activities should be included in the lesson.

5. All of the filmstrip, film, or computer program need not be used. Only the part that applies to the lesson or objectives should be used.

6. Films, filmstrips, and computer programs need to be evaluated using the same criteria for selection and utilization of other learning materials.

In summary, the library media specialist must consider many factors when planning for instruction. The age and development of the students is the first consideration. The focus for instruction should be on the strengths and abilities of the students rather than the weaknesses or the inabilities. The library media specialist has a number of strategies and materials from which to choose. It is to be hoped that a variety of strategies and materials will be used in the instructional program.

## NOTES

[1] Robert F. Biehler, *Psychology Applied to Teaching,* 2d ed. (Boston: Houghton Mifflin Company, 1974), 142, 147, 156, 159-60.

[2] Sister Edna Marie Meyers, S.C., "Teaching Library Skills to Deaf Children," *Catholic Library World* 51 (September 1979): 58-60.

[3] Walter A. Wittich, *Instructional Technology: Its Nature and Use* (New York: Harper & Row, 1973).

[4] Jerry L. Fletcher, "The Effectiveness of Simulation Games as Learning Environments," *Simulation and Games* 2 (December 1971): 425-54.

[5] Wittich, *Instructional Technology*, 586.

[6] Dwayne C. Poll, "Gaming in the Language Arts," *Elementary English* 50 (April 1973): 535-38, 548.

[7] Wittich, *Instructional Technology,* 583-84.

## BIBLIOGRAPHY

Bell, Irene W., and Jeanne E. Wieckert. *Basic Classroom Skills through Games.* Littleton, Colo.: Libraries Unlimited, Inc., 1980.

Bell, Irene W., and Jeanne E. Wieckert. *Basic Media Skills through Games.* Littleton, Colo.: Libraries Unlimited, Inc., 1979.

Biehler, Robert F. *Psychology Applied to Teaching.* 2d ed. Boston: Houghton Mifflin Company, 1974.

Cagne, Robert M. *Essentials of Learning for Instruction.* Hinsdale, Ill.: The Dryden Press, 1975.

Cyr, Don. *Teaching Your Children Photography: A Step-by-Step Guide.* Garden City, N.Y.: American Photographic Book Publishing Co., Inc., 1977.

De Renzis, Joseph J. "Reading Methods Plus Instructional System Equals Student Success." *Elementary English* 52 (May 1975): 676-78.

Fletcher, Jerry L. "The Effectiveness of Simulation Games as Learning Environments." *Simulation and Games* 2 (December 1971): 425-54.

Forte, Imogene, and Joy Mackenzie. *Nooks, Crannies & Corners: Learning Centers for Creative Classrooms.* Nashville, Tenn.: Incentive Publications, Inc., 1972.

Forte, Imogene, Mary Ann Pangle, and Robbie Tupa. *Center Stuff for Nooks, Crannies & Corners.* Nashville, Tenn.: Incentive Publications, Inc., 1973.

Galloway, Charles. *Psychology for Learning and Teaching.* New York: McGraw-Hill, Inc., 1976.

Gillespie, John T., and Diana L. Spirit. *Creating a School Media Program.* New York: R. R. Bowker Company, 1973.

Glogau, Lillian, Edmund Krause, and Miriam Wexler. *Developing a Successful Elementary School Media Center.* West Nyack, N.Y.: Parker Publishing Company, Inc., 1972.

Hart, Thomas, ed. *Instruction in School Media Center Use.* Chicago: American Library Association, 1978.

Hergenhahn, B. R. *An Introduction to Theories of Learning.* Englewood Cliffs, N.J.: Prentice-Hall, Inc., 1976.

Kaplan, Sandra Nina, Jo Ann Butom Kaplan, Sheila Kunishima Madsen, and Bette K. Taylor. *Change for Children: Ideas and Activities for Individualizing Learning.* Pacific Palisades, Calif.: Goodyear Publishing Company, Inc., 1973.

Lorton, Mary Baratta. *Workjobs: Activity-Centered Learning for Early Childhood Education.* Menlo Park, Calif.: Addison-Wesley Publishing Co., Inc. 1972.

Mayer, Mercer. *Just for You.* New York: Western Publishing Co., Inc., 1975.

McCubbin, Jacquelyn. *101 Product Ideas.* Phoenix, Ariz.: Thinking Caps, Inc., n.d.

Meyers S. C., Sister Edna Marie. "Teaching Library Skills to Deaf Children." *Catholic Library World* 51 (September 1979): 58-60.

National Association of Secondary School Principals. *Student Learning Styles: Diagnosing and Prescribing Programs.* Reston, Va.: National Association of Secondary School Principals, 1979.

Nations, Jimmy E., ed. *Learning Centers in the Classroom.* Washington, D.C.: National Education Association, 1976.

Nicholas, Donald L., and Jo Ann Crow. *Instructional Technology: Basic Media Skills Third Edition.* Manchaca, Tex.: Sterling Swift Publishing Company, 1979.

Poll, Dwayne C. "Gaming in the Language Arts." *Elementary English* 50 (April 1973): 538-38, 548.

Prostano, Emanuel T., and Joyce S. Prostano. *The School Library Media Center.* Littleton, Colo.: Libraries Unlimited, Inc., 1971.

Silverman, Eleanor. *101 Media Center Ideas.* Metuchen, N.J.: The Scarecrow Press, Inc., 1980.

Smith, Frank. *Comprehension and Learning.* New York: Holt, Rinehart, and Winston, 1975.

Walker, H. Thomas, and Paula Kay Montgomery. *Teaching Library Media Skills.* 2d ed. Littleton, Colo.: Libraries Unlimited, Inc., 1983.

Wehmeyer, Lillian Biermann. *The School Librarian as Educator.* Littleton, Colo.: Libraries Unlimited, Inc., 1976.

Wittich, Walter A. *Instructional Technology: Its Nature and Use.* New York: Harper & Row, 1973.

Wood, Nancy E. *Verbal Learning.* San Rafael, Calif.: Dimensions Publishing Co., 1969.

Zimond, Naomi K., and Regina Cicci. *Auditory Learning.* San Rafael, Calif.: Dimensions Publishing Co., 1968.

# 5 Literature Enrichment and Awareness

The literature experiences of the primary student can contribute to the child's becoming a life-long avid reader. Neither children nor adults should miss the vast array of joys and sorrows, comfort, pleasures, and beauty of the written word. While there are many books for children that are published each year that should never have been printed, there is a wealth of children's books that are of high quality. Children need to become aware of the range of human experiences and feelings that can be vicariously experienced through literature. Exposure to the many different forms of literature is imperative. Children need to hear poetry, folktales, tall tales, nonsense verse, and novels, as well as other litererary forms. They need to experience the richness of language and words. The library media specialist has the opportunity to bestow a gift on students that will last a lifetime. Providing primary students with enjoyable literary experiences enhances the student's awareness and pleasure in the many literary forms.

## PURPOSEFUL LISTENING

The need for the young student to develop listening skills is vital to development in all academic areas because so much instruction is oral in nature. While some students come to school with excellent listening skills and have already been exposed to literature and listen attentively, this is not true for all students. Some students are not familiar with the richness of the literature for the nursery set. They have not heard Mother Goose, poetry, stories, or folklore. Many young children have been conditioned not to listen unless their parents' voices reach a certain pitch. Children need to become attentive listeners. When students are required to listen to some form of literature, they should be prepared. They need a purpose for listening. A number of activities should occur before reading a story or other literary form, listening to a storyteller, viewing a film or sound filmstrip, or other listening experiences with literature.

## PREREADING ACTIVITIES

Preparation for listening should include (1) use of the students' prior knowledge to prepare them for vocabulary, plot, conflicts and resolutions, characterizations, and literary forms (young students who have a concept of the word *woods,* for example, would be helped to understand the word *forest* by the explanation that *woods* and *forest* mean the same thing); (2) development of an understanding of essential vocabulary used; (3) development of an understanding of elements of the particular literary form; and (4) provision of a purpose for listening by the instructor or by the students. Students are more attentive when they have a purpose for listening. The purpose should be stated directly. The students should be told: "Listen to this story to find..."

## ACTIVE LISTENING

In addition to providing a purpose for listening that is stated prior to reading, there are other techniques that can be used to increase listening skills. The classroom teacher and the library media specialist can read or tell stories during which the students can participate and respond. Nursery rhymes and finger plays are particularly effective vehicles for allowing students to participate in the telling. Students can respond to literature of various types in many ways.

The library media specialist can read rhyming materials and encourage students to provide the rhyming word at the end of the sentence. Nonverbal cues such as raising an eyebrow can be an indication that a response is wanted. If students are frequently asked to respond, they will become familiar with the technique and need few cues.

Very young students can be asked to provide the next word in a sentence of text. They can use pictorial clues or contextual clues to fill in the blanks. Most of the time, students will provide the correct response. If they provide a synonym or another appropriate word, students can be praised for their answer but told the author used another word. Sometimes the classroom teacher and the library media specialist may just want to say the word the author used.

Children can also provide the text for books that are "stories without words." This type of activity shifts listening to the teacher to listening to other students. In order to contribute meaningful text to these "stories without words," the student has the *need* to listen to what has been said.

Children can listen to stories and provide sound effects. For example, if the story is about farm animals, every time they hear a word that is a farm animal, they can make the sound that the animal makes. The book by Bernice Wells Carlson entitled *Listen! And Help Tell the Story* has selections that can be used. Not only is that source useful for telling stories with animal sounds, but it also provides ideas to extend listening in other situations and other sources.

Finger plays provide students with an opportunity to respond to what they hear. The activity involves them in the rhyme and gives students a reason for listening. Many young children have not had the experience of listening to this type of nursery literature. Very young students are not only learning to listen but also learning important concepts often taught in the early primary grades such as *up, down, around, in,* and *out.* Children who have these types of experiences are developing pre-reading skills.

Students can be instructed to listen to a story so that they can help act out the story after it is read. This purpose for listening is motivating for the young child. It is a rare class that does not have many students who like to take part in such role playing. This type of activity provides a meaningful reason for attentive listening, and it also provides young children with an opportunity to develop speaking skills. The child who is bashful with his or her peers may be able to talk through a puppet. While some commercial puppets may be too expensive for an individual school to purchase, they may be purchased by a central office in a school district and used by many schools on a loan basis. The library media specialist and the classroom teacher can share responsibility in this type of activity that might take place over more than just one library story time. The introduction to a story could be done by the library media specialist, the puppet making could be directed by the classroom teacher, and the acting out of the story could be done by either or both. An art teacher could become involved by helping students plan and create scenery. The library media specialist could provide instruction on the use of video equipment and students could videotape the production to share with other students.

Once children are familiar with the elements of a form of literature, they can be instructed to listen in order to identify which elements are present. Children enjoy listening to folk tales, and they can make a game out of identifying which elements of folktales are present in a particular selection. Children can be asked to listen for clues that will identify whether the story is real or make-believe. Students can be asked to raise their hand when they hear the first clue. Children need to know that when they hear "once upon a time" and "a long, long time ago" that these phrases are signals that the story is made up.

Children can be instructed to listen to the similarities and differences between similar folktales that originated in different parts of the world. Children need to have an understanding of how folktales have evolved from the oral tradition to the magnificent books that contain not only the magical words but also the illustrations that magnify the magic.

## ACTIVITIES TO FOLLOW LISTENING OR READING

Stories read by the library media specialist should not just be read and then dropped. Some follow-up activity is desirable. The activity does not have to be elaborate. If questions are used to set a purpose for listening, answering the questions is a brief follow-up activity. It can be made into a longer activity by asking students to make a class book. This activity could be continued over a period of time. For example: The students might act out a story for a video tape production. Different students would be responsible for providing the scenery, costumes, and the dialogue. Interrelating the arts is an excellent way to provide a follow-up activity; the activity can involve drama, art, music, composition, or discussion. Follow-up activities that interrelate various instructional disciplines can help not only provide more appropriate and meaningful instruction but also meet the instructional objectives of other disciplines. Interrelating the instructional disciplines also helps those who are tasked with ensuring that additions to curriculum are taught. Follow up activities do not need to be elaborate to be meaningful.

### Drama

Drama activities provide students with the opportunity to creatively express themselves and provide a change from many of the more passive activities that are frequently associated with reading and listening to literature. Dramatic activities give students the needed opportunity to orally express themselves in an appropriate manner. Many students who have difficulty expressing their own ideas before peers are able to more easily express or interpret the words of others in front of their peers. Such dramatic activities are (1) improvising a new ending for a story, (2) improvising a part of the story after making a change, (3) interpreting a story in student's own words, (4) pantomiming secret words used in a story for others to guess, (5) pantomiming the story without using words, (6) acting as animals or other unusual elements from the story, and (7) acting out a story of the past as it might happen today.

### Art

Art activities provide students with the opportunity to express themselves in a form where there are no wrong answers. A student's interpretation of a scene from a story can be accepted if he or she has reason for the work. Art activities also allow for the differences in abilities that exist between primary children. They also allow the student who may be having a difficult time with academic work to be successful with artistic efforts. Some art activities are (1) interpreting a part of a story, (2) interpreting a character's feelings in a story, (3) providing a different ending to a story with a painting or drawing, (4) creating a student-made book for others to check out of the library media center, (5) creating scenery for a class production of a story, (6) creating a collage of the various feelings, animals, or whatever from the story, and (7) creating puppets to use in recreating a story they have read or heard.

## Music

Music is another form of self-expression. While most primary children may not be able to create the melody of songs without skilled help, children can compose the lyrics of songs based on stories they hear. They can compose lyrics before they can even read by dictating their thoughts to the library media specialist, the classroom teacher, or the music teacher. With the help of the music teacher, primary students may be able to compose ballads or other types of lyrics and may be assisted in creating the melody for such lyrics. Primary students can use simple musical instruments to provide the melody. Students can create a production as a result of a story they have heard. In addition to the scenery, costumes, and dialogue, students can enhance the production by creating background music and sound effects. If the author/illustrator Beatrix Potter is being featured, the music teacher could help the students learn songs from the book *Songs of Peter Rabbit: Music by Dudley Glass* published by Frederick Warne & Co., Inc.

## Composition

Opportunities for creative composition are endless. There may not always be time for students to compose literary forms while in the library media center. Nevertheless, planning and cooperation between the classroom teacher and the library media specialist can allow students to create compositions that are of short narration or dialogue for audiovisual productions. The list of examples of composition experiences for primary students that follows is only a beginning to the many possibilities for creative expression.

1. After reading a "Pourquoi" tale, students can create their own stories explaining some natural event or occurence. Students can go one step further and tape record their story with background music and sound effects. Taping their stories gives the students an opportunity to practice oral speaking.

2. Students can write to an author or illustrator relating their thoughts about one of his or her stories.

3. Students can write a letter to one of the characters in a story.

4. Students can create different endings for stories they have heard.

5. Students can create crossword puzzles or word finds based on a story they have heard or read.

6. As a language experience approach to teaching children to read, stories without words can be used. Looking at the pictures, students dictate the story line to a parent, volunteer senior citizen, or older student. Then the students' stories can be used to teach them to read.

7. Students can make board games based on the stories they have read. Game cards can have parts of the story on them with additional instruction for movement on the game board.

8. For a language arts activity, students can compare two characters from a story. If the stories *The Tale of Peter Rabbit* and *The Tale of Benjamin Bunny* by Beatrix Potter are read, the students can compare Peter and Benjamin. This may have to be a directed activity. First, students could dictate what each of the rabbits does in the stories. Then they could tell what Peter's actions tell about him and the same for Benjamin.

9. After reading a story about a grandfather or grandmother, such as in Tomie De Paola's *Now One Foot, Now the Other* or *Watch Out for the Chicken Feet in Your Soup*, children can write a story about an experience they have had with one of their grandparents (or other relative or friend of the family).

10. After reading a story about an animal or person that dies, such as in Dick Gackenbach's *Do You Love Me?*, students can write about how they felt when an animal or person they knew died or how they think they might feel if that happened.

11. After reading poetry by Shel Silverstein, children can be encouraged to write similar poems.

12. After hearing a tall tale or other literary form, students can be encouraged to write a similar story. The story could be written in dialogue and developed into a audiovisual production that would be entered in local film festivals.

## Discussion

Discussion of stories read can be successful even with very young children. For children who are lacking in language skills or vocabulary development, the library media specialist has an opportunity to reinforce or extend what the regular classroom teacher is doing. Children from Head Start programs, primary special learning classes, and kindergarten particularly can benefit from discussing stories they have heard. Such discussions can be made more effective by setting a purpose for listening prior to hearing a story. After reading the story, the library media specialist should start the discussion using questions related to the stated purpose for listening. A variety of types of questions should be posed to students. Questions that require recalling details are quite acceptable, but certainly library media specialists or classroom teachers would not want to limit discussion to those questions. Discussion questions should generally be open-ended in nature, but students should be encouraged to support their ideas. Questions that require different kinds of thinking are desirable. Students need to make inferences. The library media specialist may ask the students why they think a character does something in the story. For example: Why does Peter Rabbit go to Mr. McGregor's garden after being warned by his mother not to go? Additionally, questions can relate students' personal experiences to the story. Each story lends itself to unique questions. Some sample questions designed as a guide for the reading of Ezra Jack Keats' *Peter's Chair* follow.

1. How do you think Peter felt when his mother told him to be quiet because of his sister?

2. How do you think Peter felt when he saw the pink baby bed?

3. Why do you think he chose to take the pictures? And the chair?

4. How do you think he felt when he didn't fit in his old chair?

5. Why do you think he hid from his mother when she called him for lunch?

6. Why do you think he asked his father to paint the chair pink?

An excellent source for additional discussion questions can be found in *Response Guides for Teaching Children's Books* by Albert B. Somers and Janet Evans Worthington.

## INTRODUCTION TO LITERARY FORM

As part of literature enrichment and awareness, young students can learn to recognize the varied forms that literature takes. The first forms they learn about are usually nursery rhymes and songs they hear at home before they start school. As part of an introduction to a story or poem, forms, types, and elements of a literary piece can be presented. For example: Prior to reading a folktale, students can be told that some people believe that folktales that were handed down from parent to child and were *told* rather than read. Some modern stories are considered folktales, but the vast majority of folktales existed before common people had access to books. Students can be led to discover common types and motifs within a literary form. A unit of study could focus on humorous tales. After reading each humorous tale, the students could relate the humorous elements.

There are a number of literary forms that can be used with primary students.

1. *Fable*. In this literary form the main character is usually an animal who acts and talks like a human. A moral lesson is unfolded in the story.

2. *Fantasy*. This is a literary form in which the imagination is used. Events that could only happen in dreams appear in fantasy.

3. *Fiction*. Fiction includes stories that are often realistic, even historical, but are totally made up. This form also includes books that tell a story without any words such as Mercer Mayer's *A Boy, a Dog & a Frog*.

4. *Folktales*. These stories may take many forms. They are thought to originate in the oral tradition as a form of recreation. The folktales changed with retelling. Because many folktales are similar and were not written down until more recent history, it is believed that they were shared among people who have migrated to other areas. Some of the common traits of folktales are simple setting, action-filled plot, indefinite time frame (as seen in such phrases as "Once upon a time"), contrasts (good against evil, wise against foolish), threeness (characters and happenings occurring in threes), and rapid conclusion. There are several types of folktales. One is called cumulative tales. These tales are stories that are repetitious yet change slightly as the story progresses and often contain rhythmical phrases. Some examples are "The Three Little Pigs," "Henny Penny," and "The Gingerbread Boy." Another type is talking animals or beasts tales. These stories have animals that talk with the wisdom or foolishness of humans. Two examples are "The Three Little Pigs" and "The Billy Goats Gruff." Humorous tales are stories in which people do silly, stupid things. Two examples are "Lazy Jack" and "The Husband Who Was to Mind the House." Realistic tales are stories in which the elements of the story are not fanciful, but realistic in nature. Religious tales are stories that contain elements of religious belief/history. One example is "The Clown of God." Romances are stories that contain love and affection between the major characters. One example is "Beauty and the Beast." Tales of magic are stories in which events happen that actually could never happen. Two examples are "Strega Nona" and "The Funny Little Woman." Character tales may be about little people (fairies, elves, etc.), for example, "The Shoemaker and the Elves"; witches, wizards, magicians, sorcerers, or fairy godmothers, for example, "Cinderella," "Strega Nona," and "Hansel and Gretel"; or giants and ogres, for example, "Jack and the Beanstalk" and "The Funny Little Woman." Pourquoi tales are stories that attempt to explain *why*. One example is "Why Mosquitoes Buzz in People's Ears."[1]

5. *Poetry*. This form includes ideas and stories that are often rhythmical and/or rhyming. Poetry creates vivid mental images and feelings with a sparsity of words.

## INTRODUCTION TO AUTHORS

Children need to become familiar with authors and illustrators. Not only do they need to learn the names of authors and illustrators, but they need to develop a desire to read or hear more of the works of a particular author or illustrator. If they are to develop into readers who avidly devour Ernest Hemingway, Ian Fleming, or other writers, students need to devour the works of authors and illustrators as young children.

During story time for primary students, the library media specialist should always make certain that the author's and illustrator's names are mentioned. If the students may have heard or seen a story by an author or illustrator before, they should be asked if they remember another story that they have heard that was written or illustrated by that person. If they cannot remember, the library media specialist may remind them. It is a good idea to feature certain authors or illustrators for a period of time. Bulletin boards and other activities can be developed to feature such artists. The classroom teacher may want to cooperate in this educational experience by featuring the same artist, providing lists of books by that author or illustrator for parents to use when selecting books from the public library. The classroom teacher also may read books by that author during regular class time. In addition to using books, films and filmstrips that feature that author/illustrator and his or her works can be shared in the library media center and the regular classroom. If two or three authors are featured each year, by the time kindergarten students reach the intermediate grades they will be ready to move into books by Judy Blume, Katherine Paterson, C. S. Lewis, Madeleine L'Engle, John Christopher, Shel Silverstein, Ellen Raskin, Beverly Cleary, Mary Stolz, and Elaine Konigsburg and look for such illustrators as Trina Schart Hyman.

Featuring an author/illustrator for a month or more provides the students with an opportunity to learn about that author's style and subject matter. When featuring an author/illustrator, the stories should be read and other activities should be planned as well. Some sample activities that primary students can do are given in chapter 8. When an author/illustrator is featured, library media skills of locating needed materials and the organization of the library media center should be taught informally to primary students. When students have a need to locate a material they want, the instruction is much more meaningful. When an author/illustrator is featured, many students will want to locate additional books by this author/illustrator. Additional copies or several paperback copies may be required to support the needs of the students. The class may want to send a letter to the author/illustrator and this is a good motivator. The regular classroom teacher may want to include letter writing skills as part of the language arts curriculum at this time. The letter writing skills should be taught at this time because of the student's need rather than waiting to teach these skills within the consecutive order of a teacher's language textbook. While an author/illustrator may not be able to respond to the class letter, some publishing companies send either a picture or other material such as a poster by the author/illustrator. Centering the various instructional objectives around a featured author/illustrator is a good example of the integration of instruction.

The timing for featuring author/illustrators can be approached from three directions: (1) level of difficulty of material, (2) seasonal considerations, and (3) related curriculum.

At the beginning of the year, very young children who have had limited experience in school or in the library media center may do well to read short narratives that contain concepts familiar to their lives. Authors such as John Burningham or Marie Hall Ets may be used at this time. These authors use simple words that are repeated. The concepts developed are not difficult. After a number of first-grade students have started to learn to read and are ready for easy-to-read materials, authors such as Edith Hurd, Syd Hoff, and Anne Rockwell may be featured.

It may be desirable to feature an author/illustrator during the month of his or her birthday. If Maurice Sendak is featured with first-grade students, the month of September may be desirable because of the book *Alligators All Around.* Students can be helped to commit to memory the poem for each month. The library media specialist can teach the children the September poem as a surprise for their classroom teacher. Other months could be continued by their classroom teacher.

If Russell and Lillian Hoban are featured, the months of November and December may be selected because of the book *Arthur's Christmas Cookies.* In cooperation with either the classroom teacher or the art teacher, the students may make their families the same Christmas decorations as Arthur made. This is another example of how the library media specialist and other staff members can plan and work cooperatively.

An author/illustrator whose work centers on science materials may be useful in the spring when students can satisfy their curiosity about the changes in nature. After other authors/illustrators have been featured, a comparison of the authors/illustrators can be made. Questions such as these can be posed to primary students.

1. How are the illustrators' works different? (One may have used bolder colors, different materials to create the illustrations, or different subject matters.)

2. After students have heard both Mercer Mayer's *There's a Nightmare in My Closet,* and Maurice Sendak's *Where the Wild Things Are,* they can be asked: How are the monsters alike/different? Do you think the stories were the boy's dream or fantasy? Do you think either of the illustrators was frightened of monsters as a child? Why do you think that?

In summary, literature enrichment and awareness activities are an excellent opportunity to integrate language arts curriculum objectives with library media skills objectives. The traditional story time for primary students should go beyond the library media specialist's merely reading or telling stories. When students hear stories by Ezra Jack Keats, they should also learn how they can locate other books by Keats and how call numbers are composed. Story time activities can integrate language arts activities, library media skills activities, and interrelated arts activities.

## NOTES

[1] Zena Sutherland, Dianne L. Monson, and May Hill Arbuthnot, *Children & Books* (Glenview, Ill.: Scott, Foresman & Co., 1981), 161-66.

## BIBLIOGRAPHY

Baker, Augusta, and Ellin Greene. *Storytelling: Art and Technique.* New York: R. R. Bowker Company, 1977.

Borba, Michele, and Dan Ungaro. *Bookends.* Carthage, Ill.: Good Apple, Inc., 1982.

Bauer, Caroline Feller. *Handbook for Storytellers.* Chicago: American Library Association, 1977.

Carlson, Bernice Wells. *Listen! And Help Tell the Story.* New York: Abingdon Press, 1965.

Glogau, Lillian, Edmund Krause, and Miriam Wexler. *Developing a Successful Elementary School Media Center.* West Nyack, N.Y.: Parker Publishing Company, Inc., 1972.

Johnson, Ferne, ed. *Start Early for an Early Start.* Chicago: American Library Association, 1976.

Mealy, Virginia T. *Hand in Hand: From Word Power to Thought-Power through Picture Books.* O'Fallon, Mo.: Book Lures, Inc., 1982.

Peterson, Carolyn Sue, and Brenny Hall. *Story Programs: A Source Book of Materials.* Metuchen, N.J.: The Scarecrow Press, Inc., 1980.

Silverman, Eleanor. *101 Media Center Ideas.* Metuchen, N.J.: The Scarecrow Press, Inc., 1980.

Somers, Albert B., and Janet Evans Worthington. *Response Guides for Teaching Children's Books.* Urbana, Ill.: National Council of Teachers of English, 1979.

Sutherland, Zena, Dianne L. Monson, and May Hill Arbuthnot. *Children & Books,* 6th ed. Glenview, Ill.: Scott, Foresman & Co., 1981.

Wehmeyer, Lillian Biermann. *The School Librarian as Educator.* Littleton, Colo.: Libraries Unlimited, Inc., 1976.

# 6  Evaluation, Assessment, and Record Keeping

Evaluation of learning is not intended to mean *testing of students*. Evaluation of learning is meant to be interpreted in the broadest context to include assessment of the total program or system including

- objectives

- diagnostic tools and plans

- learning materials

- instruction

The total library media skills program needs to be continually assessed.

## OBJECTIVES

The information explosion has made it necessary for each individual to seek information to satisfy particular needs. Whether a need is basic to survival, such as reading classified advertisements to find housing, or recreational in nature, such as locating a tennis club in the telephone directory, students need to become information-seeking citizens. When assessing the objectives for student learning, the library media specialist needs to ask such questions as: Are objectives based on the needs/abilities of the students? Are objectives appropriate for age/development of the students?

## DIAGNOSTIC TOOLS AND PLANS

Diagnosis of student abilities is a necessary step in the total system. A student who does not have facility with use of the alphabet cannot be expected to learn to use a dictionary. Diagnosis of student abilities is part of instruction. Since most diagnostic information gathered at the primary level is from observation and the classroom teacher, the library media specialist needs to (1) develop keen observational skills, and (2) actively plan with classroom teachers and other resource teachers.

Development of written assessments needs to be done carefully. Written assessments need to match objectives.

OBJECTIVE:  The student will locate the index of an encyclopedia.

ASSESSMENT: Using a picture of a set of encyclopedias, the student will identify which volume is the index.

This assessment does not match the objective because the objective states the student will *locate* the index while the assessment asks student to *identify* the index. The assessment for this objective should require an instructor's *observation* of the student's locating in the library media center the index to an encyclopedia. Pencil and paper assessment for that objective is not appropriate.

Here is an example of a match between objective and assessment:

OBJECTIVE:  The student will use the table of contents to locate information.

ASSESSMENT: Given a table of contents, the student will write the page number on which chapter two begins and turn the pages to that chapter.

During pretesting, the library media specialist does not need to be concerned with whether the skill has been taught. When paper and pencil assessments are used in a pretesting situation, it is quite appropriate to let students know (1) they are not expected to know all the answers, and (2) that the assessment is to find out what skills the student has. It is a tool to improve instruction.

It is essential that the library media specialist determine whether students have the skills or learnings that are needed or embedded within a task and whether they are able to perform certain tasks before instruction. Giving instruction on how to use an encyclopedia before the student can locate an encyclopedia is not appropriate.

## ASSESSMENT OF STUDENT LEARNING

The library media specialist needs to assess student learning. This should be an on-going process rather than a once or twice a year administering of a pencil and paper test. At the primary level, most assessment should be done by observation of behavior to identify whether students are able to accomplish tasks. While a student is trying to learn to use a dictionary, for example, the library media specialist can observe whether the student is using guide words, whether he or she has difficulty finding the section where an entry word should be found. There should be no emphasis on testing at the primary level. Assessments should be looked at as diagnostic tools.

## ASSESSMENT OF INSTRUCTION

Assessment of instruction is important so that students learn because of, rather than in spite of, instruction. Assessment of instruction may be most difficult because of the personal involvement. Sometimes it is difficult to evaluate oneself. Someone else may be called in to evaluate one instructional situation or the total instructional program. It would be hoped that other people involved such as library media supervisors or principals would look at such assessment with the idea of improving student learning. It is often difficult to have someone else assess instructional performance because such assessments can be looked upon as threatening and critical. Others may be sensitive to such feelings and include many positive comments as "suggestions." The evaluator should focus on one or two priorities that need attention rather than bombarding the library media specialist with too many suggestions. To sum up, such an assessment should be viewed as a learning experience rather than criticism. Other methods of assessing instructional performance are student evaluations and videotapes for self-assessment.

Self-evaluation checklists of the instructional program are also helpful. At the end of each year, or even more often, it is important to look at what is being done and what needs to be changed. A comparison from previous self-evaluations is useful to see changes and trends.

There are a number of criteria for evaluating instruction. For example, during planning does the library media specialist (1) use objectives, (2) plan instruction with classroom teacher, (3) know subject area curriculum, (4) integrate media skills into subject area curriculum, (5) use information on student skills, and (6) utilize assessments as diagnostic tools? During teaching, does the library media specialist (1) use objectives, (2) inform students of objectives, (3) use a variety of instructional resources, (4) modify instructional strategies to meet student needs, (5) provide appropriate learning activities, (6) build new learnings based on obtained skills, (7) continually assess student learnings, (8) adjust strategies according to student needs, and (9) recognize student achievement?

## ASSESSMENT OF LEARNING MATERIALS

Unlike many curriculum areas, there is not a wealth of materials available for teaching library media skills. Many library media specialists create materials geared to the needs of their students. Some school districts are also creating learning materials that are distributed systemwide to help teach library media skills. Sharing of learning materials that match the academic curriculum of each particular school system can be of immense assistance. When purchasing commercially prepared materials, evaluation of such materials before purchase is imperative. Some criteria to use when purchasing commercially prepared materials include

- Does it meet the objective?

- Is it readable?

- Is it durable?

- Would it appeal to the student user?

- Will it become dated quickly?

- Is its use time-effective?

- Is it suitable for the age/development of students?

- Does it support subject area curriculum?

- Can the student use it without assistance?

- Is it cost-effective?

- Are directions/instructions simple and clear?

- Is it accurate?

- How often will it be used?

- Is instruction effective?

- Are illustrations/examples clear and understandable?

Materials may not measure up to all criteria but still may be worth purchasing. For example, a learning material that may not support subject area curriculum but does an excellent job meeting most other criteria can be used as an introductory material. As budgets are tightened, it is imperative to spend money wisely. Materials can often be examined prior to purchase. The cost of sending back unwanted materials may be money well spent. While reviews of materials and the opinions of fellow library media specialists may be valuable, personal inspection of materials is very important.

This is especially true with the cost of many multimedia materials. The materials may be excellent in quality and money value, but they might not meet the needs of the student users.

Students, the classroom teacher, and the library media specialist need to assess learning materials. Students are able to decide whether the materials were clear and easy to understand. The library media specialist needs to evaluate learning materials before purchase, during and after production of teacher-made materials, prior to use with students, during use with students, and following use with students.

## METHODS OF RECORD KEEPING

Record keeping need not be a burden and can provide valuable information about the students. A variety of methods to record students' progress and achievement can be employed ranging from a simple class checklist requiring a pencil to computer management.

The class checklist that closely resembles a grade book (fig. 6.1) can be employed to note progress, completion, or achievement. Students' names are listed. When a student completes a task or demonstrates a skill, a check mark can be noted. This method gives limited information but does not require much effort.

| | Operate Rec. Player | Operate Overhead Proj. | Operate F.S. Prev. | Operate F.S. Proj. | Animal Dict. L.P. | Card Cat. Adv. | Search and Find | Map Skills |
|---|---|---|---|---|---|---|---|---|
| Bobby A. | ✓ | | | | ✓ | | | |
| Janey B. | ✓ | ✓ | | | ✓ | ✓ | | |
| Donna D. | | | | | | | | |
| Linda G. | ✓ | ✓ | ✓ | | ✓ | ✓ | | |
| Albert K. | ✓ | ✓ | | | | | | |
| Kimberly M. | ✓ | | | | | | | |

Fig. 6.1. Sample class checklist.

Another method of noting progress is the use of a 6" x 8" index card (fig. 6.2). Each block can represent a learning center, lap pack, or demonstration of a skill.

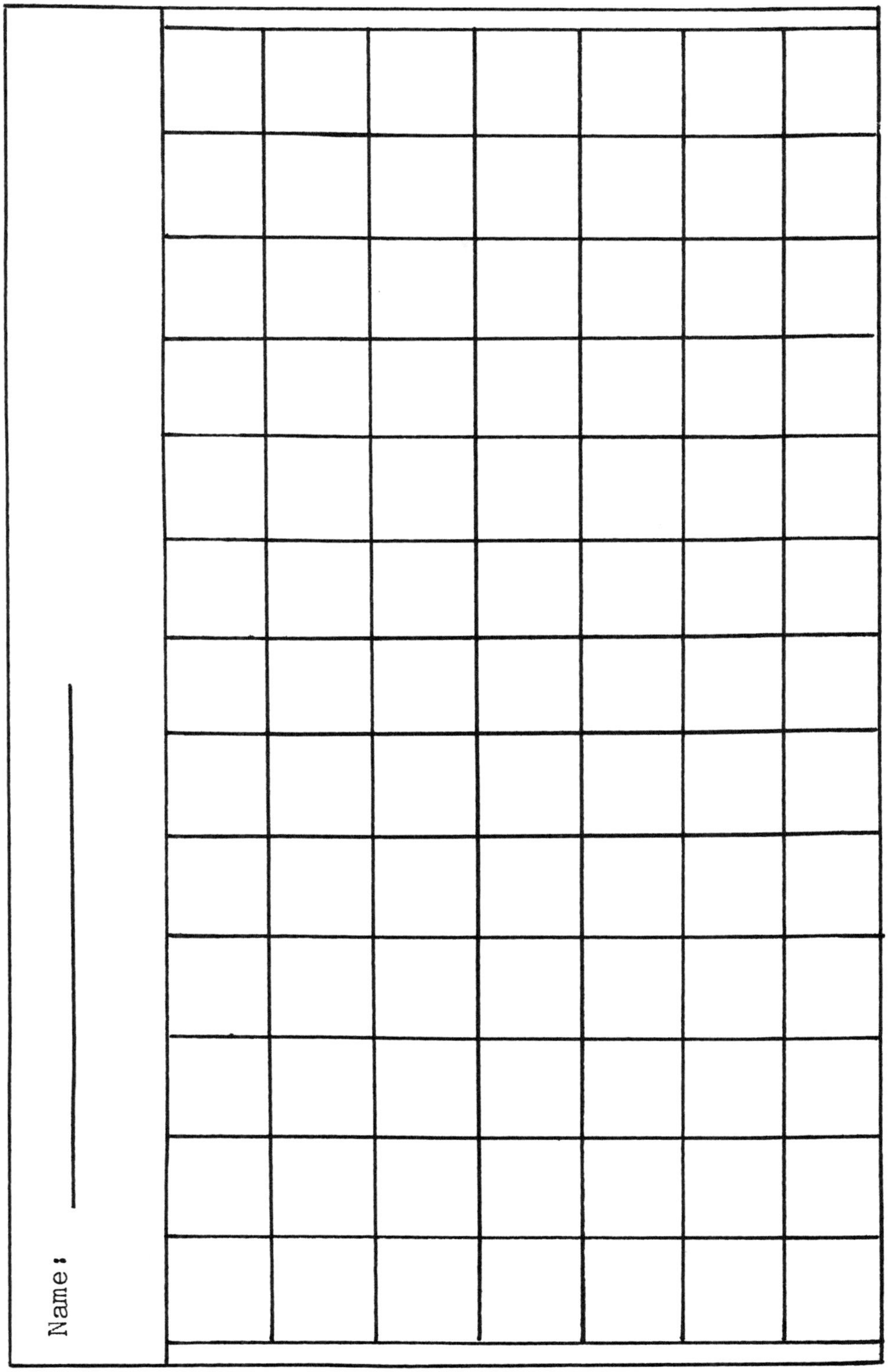

Name: _____

Fig. 6.2. Sample progress card kept on a student from grade to grade.

Several keys (fig. 6.3) that identify what each square represents can be made. It is a good idea to keep keys in several places just in case the original is accidentally lost.

Name: _____

| | Operate | | | | | | | | |
|---|---|---|---|---|---|---|---|---|---|
| **f.s. preview** | | | | | Mini centers | | | | |
| **opaque proj.** | | | | Ency. Use | | | | | |
| **VTR** | | | | | | | | | |
| **16mm proj.** | | | | | | | | | |
| **record player** | | | | | | | | | |
| **f.s. proj.** | | | | | | | | | |
| **cassette recorder** | | | | | | | | | |
| **Make transparency** | | | | | | | | | |
| | | | Folk-tale center | | | Learn to use L.M.C. a | Animal Dic. Lap Pack | card cat. adv.#1 | |
| | | | | | | Learn to use L.M.C. b | Search and Find | card cat. adv.#2 | Map skills 1-15 |
| | | | | | | | Dive into Dict. | Box 1-10 | Box 11-20 |
| **Pet computer center** | | | | | | | | Box 21-30 | Box 31-40 |
| | | Tall tales center | | | | Find it fast | | | |
| | | Using Ref. Coll. | | | | | | Research Skills Lap Pack | |

Fig. 6.3. Sample key to a progress card.

This card can be used for the student all through elementary school. Different colored pens can be used to differentiate school years (one year could be marked with a red pen, the following year with a black pen, etc.). A diagonal slash can be made on the block that represents the current activity or skill the student is working on and the starting date can be placed on top of the slash (fig. 6.4). Another slash and date on the bottom could be used to designate the completion date (fig. 6.5).

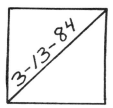

Fig. 6.4. Sample marking for date started.

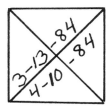

Fig. 6.5. Sample marking for date completed.

This keeps a record of completion, but it also gives information about how long each student needed to complete a task or learn a skill. Other notes could be placed on the back of this card. If the library media specialist is ever going to be gone for several weeks or months, he or she could go through student cards and make the first slash on each student's card to indicate the next activity the student is to do. That way, the student's program can continue while the substitute library media specialist is teaching. It is also useful to the classroom teacher. Since this card can follow each student from the time formal instruction is started, it can also be a diagnostic tool. A glance at the student's card shows whether the student has or has not demonstrated a skill or competence. Additional information can be added. For example: When a new student enters the school in the middle of the year, questioning of the student may reveal that he or she has had extensive work in using the card catalog. If the last activity of the card catalog center is a posttest type activity and the student can demonstrate proficiency on it, he or she could receive credit for the whole center. A notation of only doing one part can also be made (fig. 6.6).

Fig. 6.6. Sample marking for part of activity completed.

For keeping a record of activities that have many parts, the classroom teacher and/or the library media specialist may want to employ slips to record progress (fig. 6.7).

| | Date | Initials | To Do |
|---|---|---|---|
| Name: _____ | | | |
| Activity: _____ | | | |
| Date Started: _____ | | | |
| 1 | | | |
| 2 | | | |
| 3 | | | |
| 4 | | | |
| 5 | | | |
| 6 | | | |
| 7 | | | |
| 8 | | | |
| 9 | | | |
| 10 | | | |
| 11 | | | |
| 12 | | | |
| 13 | | | |
| 14 | | | |
| 15 | | | |
| 16 | | | |
| 17 | | | |
| 18 | | | |
| 19 | | | |
| 20 | | | |

Fig. 6.7. Sample slips used to monitor progress on individual activities.

The student would fill in his/her name. The classroom teacher or the library media specialist would fill in the activity and date started. If there are five assignments, the library media specialist could draw a line through number six. If there are five assignments and a quest activity, a *Q* could be written over the six and a line drawn through number seven. The column labeled "To Do" can be used to note any work the student needs to do over that is discovered when the classroom teacher or the library media specialist checks the student's work. This provides a record of the difficulties the student encountered. This slip could be used for a variety of activities. Specific slips following the same format could be made for specific activities or centers depending on the need (fig. 6.8).

| Name: | | |
|---|---|---|
| Equipment | Demonstrated Competency in Use | |
| | Date | Initials |
| Record Player | | |
| Filmstrip Projector | | |
| Filmstrip Previewer | | |
| 16-mm Projector | | |
| | | |

Fig. 6.8. Sample progress slip for a specific need.

These slips give recognition for tasks completed or for demonstrated competency. Signing and dating a slip when a task has been accomplished gives the student a written pat on the back and an opportunity to give verbal recognition. The slips also provide a means of monitoring progress. Also, the student's absences can be noted on the side of the slip. This helps the library media specialist determine whether a student has missed work time or has needed more time to complete an assignment.

In summary, the classroom teacher, library media specialist, and the students should be continuously evaluating and assessing student learning, instruction, and learning materials. The evaluation and assessment should occur before, during, and after instruction. Evaluation and assessment should be a part of a continuous cycle.

Record keeping should be kept simple and should not be time-consuming. Record-keeping devices can provide information as to what the student has achieved, where difficulty was encountered, and how long the student needed before demonstrating proficiency with the task. Additionally, record-keeping devices can be written recognition of the student's accomplishments.

## BIBLIOGRAPHY

Galloway, Charles. *Psychology for Learning and Teaching.* New York: McGraw-Hill, Inc., 1976.

Prostano, Emanuel T., and Joyce S. Prostano. *The School Library Media Center.* Littleton, Colo.: Libraries Unlimited, Inc., 1971.

Walker, H. Thomas, and Paula K. Montgomery. *Teaching Library Media Skills,* 2d ed. Littleton, Colo.: Libraries Unlimited, Inc., 1983.

Wehmeyer, Lillian Biermann. *The School Librarian as Educator.* Littleton, Colo.: Libraries Unlimited, Inc., 1976.

# Part II

# 7 Creating and Storing Learning Materials

## STEPS FOR CREATING LEARNING MATERIALS

In creating learning materials several steps may be taken to complete usable materials that will contribute to the learning process.

1. Decide what the instructional objectives are. In many school systems, library media specialists have a set of instructional objectives for teaching library media skills to students from kindergarten to grade twelve. If a list of objectives for library media skills is already completed, a decision needs to be made as to which objectives will be focused upon. If such a list is not available, objectives should be developed. Stated learning objectives give direction to the process of creating any instructional activities or materials.

2. Get an idea of a topic or curriculum correlation. Some time needs to be spent jotting down possible ideas that might serve as a basis upon which to develop learning materials and activities. This paper should not be thrown away since it may be a source for future learning materials or centers. Doing an inventory of what teaching materials are already available and comparing that inventory to the instructional objectives for each grade level may help to develop long-range plans for creating instructional experiences and materials. This might generate a list for future learning materials.

3. Gather anything related to the topic or type of material. Bibliographies, old dittos, any commercially prepared materials, filmstrips, films, overhead transparencies, actual materials (for a learning center on encyclopedias, some volumes, the index, and any materials that the publisher might have produced, such as study guides or advertising pamphlets—anything remotely connected, would need to be gathered). Other library media specialists can be a resource; they can share what they have done on the topic or type of material. Ideas and resources need to be collected.

   A file on library media skills topics should be started. This file system could contain dittos, materials received at meetings or from other library media specialists, commercially prepared materials, and other items. One file might contain pictures cut out of vendor catalogs that might be useful later when constructing learning materials. Some sample file folder labels might be Card Catalog, Center Ideas, Dictionary, Film Production, Index, Periodicals, Pictures from Withdrawn Books, Pictures for Learning Materials, Pictures of Authors/Illustrators, Table of Contents, and U-Film Production.

4. Examine commercially prepared materials. An evaluation must be made of materials already available either in the individual library media center or on loan from some central source within the school system. Notes should be made as to what may be useful in the future. Commercially prepared materials may be of use either by themselves or by incorporation with instructional materials that have already been or will be developed. Journals and other acquisition sources may indicate commerically prepared materials that might be useful. It may be worthwhile to order such materials for examination. Some school systems have a union catalog and are able to provide information as to whether other schools have a particular item. Borrowing the material will help the library media specialist decide whether that particular item meets the stated objectives and is worth purchasing.

5. Allow thinking time. A few days should be allowed just to let ideas stir around. Paper should be kept handy to jot notes as ideas develop. Some of the best ideas may come while driving in the car to work or perhaps while standing in the shower. This may seem like wasted time, but it will not be. Time constraints or excitement to get on with the task may make thinking time next to impossible.

6. Outline or plan activities. Decisions as to what types and/or sequence of activities for students need to be made. Ask such questions as What type of activity(ies) will best meet the instructional objectives? and What type of learning materials will assist the students in learning the objectives?

    Learning activities and/or materials should not be limited to worksheets. Activities can include viewing filmstrips, creating some type of media, creating a computer program, and so forth. Some examples of activities that primary students can do include

- matching
- role-playing
- pantomime
- chronological order (using pictures)
- chronological order (using phrases or sentences)
- art work such as working with clay, paint, or crayon
- rebus
- map work
- mazes
- crossword puzzles
- dot-to-dot
- jigsaw puzzles
- fill-in-the-blank
- hidden pictures
- make/use game boards (either pictorial or written)

- paper dolls

- flannel board

- making a class or individual diorama

- making puppets or masks

- using puppets or masks

Some examples of instructional formats primary students can use include

- gaming

- models made by students (students learn to use a card catalog by creating a class card catalog)

- booklets or lap packs (Primary students enjoy having a booklet that they have completed. Many students want to take them home to play school when they are completed.)

- learning centers

- task cards

- group discussion

- use of media

- demonstration

- every pupil response

A decision needs to be made as to how many lessons or activities are needed. For example, if a learning center is planned on the use of a particular dictionary, the objectives for the students may include ability to use guide words, finding entry words, finding pronunciations, and finding appropriate definitions. One activity for each objective may be adequate. Then, again, the students may need review and/or practice in applying alphabetical rules that would add another activity. There is no set number of activities for a learning center, lap pack, or other form of instructional materials. Additionally, the number of activities in a center is not the determining factor as to how many of those activities each student does. All students may not do all activities. Activity number one may be a pretest. If a student can successfully complete activity one, credit may be given to the student for doing the whole center. If the pretest is diagnostic in nature, the student may be assigned to do only those activities that would help in the areas he or she had difficulty. The last activity may be used as a posttest. A new student who states that he or she has had instruction on a given topic may be given the last activity as an assessment of his or her ability.

A center on the use of the card catalog may contain activities on (1) finding the guide letters on the outside of the drawers, (2) using the guide cards on the inside of the drawers, (3) finding author cards, (4) finding subject cards, (5) finding title cards, and (6) applying what has been learned and finding information on all types of cards. If a student can successfully find all types of information except those dealing with title cards, the student could be assigned to do only those activities that deal with finding and using title cards.

7. Make activities, booklets, question sheets. Before actually making materials, determine

- What elements need to be included?

- How many students will be using the materials?

- What type of learning materials will be most effective?

- How can needed information/instruction be provided?

- How will students' work be evaluated?

Remember to save the original masters of learning materials.

Consideration must be given to the various parts that need to be included in most learning materials such as a title, stated purpose(s) or objective(s), directions, and evaluation for learning.

After completing any learning materials, they need to be checked to make sure that

- language is simple and understandable

- materials are in fact meeting the stated objective(s) or purpose(s)

- activities are appropriate for the age, needs, and/or interests of the students

Directions need to be simple and clear, and the understanding and reading levels of the students who will be using the center need to be considered. As in all areas of the curriculum, the library media specialist must be a teacher of reading. The concept being taught may be easily understood by the student, providing the vocabulary used is recognizable and understandable. That is not to say that "big" words cannot be used with primary students; it merely means that they must be taught how to recognize and understand them. The structure and length of the sentences need to be considered; a complex sentence or one that is too long could be a barrier to learning. If possible and appropriate, the types of activities should be varied, made progressively more difficult, and allow for creativity and individuality. While it may not always be possible or desirable, these guidelines should be considered when creating learning materials.

The number of students who will be using these learning materials at any one time needs to be considered. Multiple copies of the activity are not needed if only one student will be using it. However, if small groups will be using it, multiple copies of the activity as well as adequate additional materials (e.g., dictionaries, atlases, almanacs) will be needed. Additional choices within an exercise may be needed because of the number of students and the number of support materials available. This type of problem can be minimized by borrowing or purchasing multiple copies of the support material. If an encyclopedia is being used, the same task(s) can be accomplished in different volumes. All five third-grade students working on an encyclopedia center with one set of encyclopedias can perform such tasks as using guide words and the parts of an article, using main headings and subheadings, reading captions, and locating information. The instructor simply must provide them with individual topics that require five separate volumes (perhaps using articles about Mexico, Japan, Ghana, India, or Argentina).

When planning activities or booklets, an effort should be made to save materials and time. If students are able to write answers on their own paper rather than on ditto sheets, materials do not need constant replenishing and students' papers can be corrected easily. With early primary students this is not possible or desirable.

Originals of learning materials should not be used. A file folder can be used to store the masters for each learning center, lap pack, or other type of learning material. It is also a good idea to file at least one spare copy of any additional materials used. If a particular map or issue of a periodical is part of the learning materials, it is often difficult, if not impossible, to locate duplicates in a year or so if the original is lost or misplaced. Keeping an original copy of all learning materials is a good idea for several reasons: Replacements are easier to make if the originals are available. Copies for other library media specialists are easier to provide. Corrections can be made on masters. Originals can serve as models.

It can be heartbreaking to discover an error. But, that is not as devastating as discovering your only copy is laminated and in a center. Masters that you save can also be used to serve as models for similar learning materials at other grade levels. A learning center on the use of encyclopedias for third-grade students would include many of the skills that would be used in a center for fifth- or sixth-grade students. At the advanced level, some skills still need additional reinforcement, while others could be eliminated or added. When duplicating copies from the masters, it is wise to get good quality photocopies. Inferior copies look inferior and are often more difficult to read. Copies made from thermal copiers often turn brown when laminated.

Consideration should be given to the method of instruction. With a learning center, for example, there are several ways that instructional information can be provided. An instructional booklet can be included in the center that guides the student through that center. A section within each activity may provide instruction (e.g., at the top of each activity sheet instructional information may be provided). Sections within the center may provide the instructional information.

There are a number of ways to evaluate student work. Students can check their own work if answers are provided. This method does not always work well if questions/tasks are open-ended. Such questions or tasks can be evaluated by the library media specialist or by the library media specialist and the student. Both the library media specialist and the student need to be involved at some point.

8. Plan layout. Planning should ensure that the learning materials are easy for the student to understand, use, and follow. The library media specialist needs to consider how and which resources can be used to make the learning materials appealing and attractive.

The library media specialist does *not* need to be an artist to make learning centers or any other learning materials attractive and appealing. But, a few tricks are needed. Illustrations saved from vendors' catalogs and advertising pamphlets can be invaluable for making a learning center attractive. If a learning center is being made to feature an author, illustrations from the author's books can be used by cutting up books that have been discarded because of their condition. Frequently, book vendor catalogs have pictures of authors as well as illustrations from their books. If the library media specialist plans to make centers that feature particular authors, an author file for pictures of those authors and illustrations from their books should be started. A file of pictures for future learning centers can make a difficult task easier. Another tool that can prove invaluable for making activity sheets, learning centers, and other learning materials attractive is the use of copyright free graphics. Many large school systems have such graphics available in either a graphic department or a center where teachers can go to produce learning materials. Usually a photocopy is made of the original master. From there, the photocopy can be cut out and used directly. If a larger graphic is needed, an overhead transparency can be made from the photocopy. An overhead projector can be used to blow it up. Many books are available for learning the technique of doing graphics and doing layouts.

Attractive lettering can be accomplished in several ways. A file of lettering masters can be started. If a black copy is available, an overhead transparency can be made. By using the transparency and an overhead projector, letters can be enlarged for titles. Letters can also be traced from the transparencies for titles by using the stage of an overhead projector as a light box. To make neat, large lettering for activity sheets, written directions, or titles and labels, a primary typewriter is useful. Lettering guides that are available in stationary/office supply stores can also be used. There are special pens that are generally used with lettering guides. A very sharp pencil also can be used with lettering guides. Then, the pencil lines can be traced using fine line magic markers. Experience using various felt tip markers is needed to decide which brand gives the best results. Some give a sharp line, while others tend to bleed. Time spent on making the center look professional is well worth the effort.

With little or no artistic talent, learning materials can be made attractive. Student helpers, parents, or senior volunteers can color any illustrations before materials are assembled and/or laminated. Depending on the paper used and what the finished product is expected to look like, colored pencils are often preferable to other media because mistakes are easy to repair (an eraser does not remove magic marker or crayon marks) and pencil marks do not bleed when laminated. For appearance, coordination of the colors should be considered for the panels of learning centers (mounting boards), the materials on which worksheets and titles are mounted, and titles and other graphics used. Consultation with an art teacher or person with similar talents for advice can be useful.

9. Field test instructional materials with students. Testing learning materials with a small group of students is essential. As the materials are used, notes should be made of any problems or mistakes encountered. Anything that would be useful in the future should also be noted. Students can provide valuable insight into what works and what does not work. Some items may need to be expanded, eliminated, or revised. Additional topics may need to be added because students may lack needed skills.

10. Revise instructional materials if needed. Revisions that are needed after a field testing with a group of students must be made before the learning materials are made into their final form. After revisions are made, learning materials should be evaluated again.

From time to time, minor revision may be made. As almanacs, atlases, and encyclopedias are updated, revisions to learning materials need to be made. A good example of a needed revision would be on any instructional materials made for telephone directories prior to 1980. Any learning materials made before this time do not reflect the latest modifications in this reference tool. Learning materials should be clearly marked to indicate which edition of a resource is to be used. As school objectives change, modifications may also be made to learning materials. If a master file of learning materials is kept, revisions will probably be much easier to accomplish than starting from scratch.

11. Make it sturdy to last. Laminate learning centers when possible. The first and last page of lap packs and other activity sheets last much longer if they are laminated. If the school does not have a laminator (not a dry mount press used as a laminator), perhaps the parent-teacher association would buy one or the school could sponsor a fund-raising activity such as a book fair to purchase one. It may seem like an extravagance, but once the school has one, the staff will wonder how they ever got along without one. For most schools, a laminator that takes an eighteen-inch roll of film is probably ideal. There are techniques a laminator representative can demonstrate for laminating items that are almost thirty-six inches wide. Many school systems have laminating facilities available in

a central location. Since learning centers can last years and be used by hundreds of students, it is well worth the effort to make the materials as durable as possible. Some learning centers are such work horses that they may need occasional replacement. Parent or senior citizen volunteers may be able to copy a center.

Individual worksheets may be made more durable by mounting them on railroad board or other sturdy material before laminating (see fig. 7.1). Making the work or activity sheets at least one-half inch smaller all around than the board on which they are mounted will make them more durable and attractive. If two sheets are sandwiched and the edge of the laminating gets worn, the pages can easily separate. Numbers noting the sequence of activities should be placed on the body of the activity or worksheet. When laminating worksheets, it is a good idea not to trim right to the edge. Leave at least one-eighth of an inch around the edge.

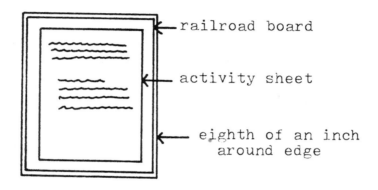

**Fig. 7.1. Laminated activity sheet.**

## METHODS OF STORING LEARNING MATERIALS

Several factors need to be considered when planning for the storage of learning materials: (1) use of space, (2) accessibility, and (3) organization.

Most library media centers do not have adequate space for storing learning materials. When purchasing or producing learning materials, an important consideration is the space they will occupy when in use and when being stored. Different methods of storage can be used with different types of learning materials.

Lap packs can be stacked in a pile and stored on shelves in the library media center or stored in a file cabinet when not in use for an extended period. File folders (learning materials that are single concept in nature and are produced on file folders) can be stored in a box or in a file cabinet. Kits/filmstrips/slide tape productions can be stored with similar media in the library media center. Learning centers (stand up boards) can be folded and stored standing up between file cabinets, against a wall, or in a large box that would allow easy access. A set of mini-centers intended to be used as a set could be housed in a box separate from other learning centers. Task cards (separate cards intended to be used one at a time) can be stored in a box that has been covered and has appropriate, attractive labels that easily identify the contents. These could then be placed on a shelf in the library media center. Individual activity cards can be housed in file folders in a file cabinet or in separate envelopes. Games (commercially made or teacher-made library media skills games) can be housed in appropriate containers (boxes, folders, etc.) and can be treated in the same manner as other games in the library media center.

Learning materials need to be readily accessible to students, the library media specialist, and classroom teachers. If students are expected to be responsible for their own learning, they need to be able to retrieve needed materials to complete assignments. Second-grade students who come to to the library media center in a small group to work on a dictionary lap pack should be able to retrieve their own papers and the needed materials (dictionary lap pack, dictionary, etc.) to complete the assignment. If learning materials are difficult to retrieve by the student, the library media specialist, or the classroom teacher, the learning materials may be used less or not at all and valuable resources (materials and time) will have been wasted.

There are several ways to organize learning materials: by grade level, by subject, by type of learning material, or by a combination of these. The important considerations for organizing learning materials are accessibility and available space. What would work best in one library media center may not work best in another. Teaching styles, space available, and layout of the library media center are some factors in determining how to organize learning materials. Problems may exist with whatever organizational pattern is selected. If grade level is used, some materials are or can be used with several grade levels and various types of learning materials are not compatible for storing together. One hopes a variety of learning materials will be used and produced. Depending on the situation, the best organizational pattern may be a combination.

# 8
# *Sample Learning Activities*

The seven activities that follow represent samples that may be used as developed or as models for preparing activities as noted in chapter 4, "Identification of Instructional Strategies." Each instructional activity has been prepared for a given grade level. These are, however, easily modified. These activities may be used by both the classroom teacher and the library media specialist.

The first activity, *Just for You* Activity, represents a whole class activity in which kindergarten or first-grade students make a model book. It is also an activity to follow the reading of a book.

The Student-made Card Catalog represents a small group or whole class activity for first-grade students to make a model of the card catalog.

The Ezra Jack Keats Center represents a learning center appropriate for use with a small group or whole class of first-grade students.

The Animal Dictionary Lap Pack represents a lap pack for use with students in the second or third grade. This lap pack can be used by an individual student, a small group of students, or a whole class.

The Spain: Using an Encyclopedia activity could be made into a booklet, task cards, or individual worksheets. It is designed to integrate library media skills objectives with third-grade objectives in the social studies unit "Communities of the World."

The Novel Unit for *Charlotte's Web* is designed to be used with a small group of third-grade gifted and talented students and/or very able readers. This unit incorporates interrelated arts activities.

The Search and Find activity is designed for individual students or a small group of students from the third or fourth grade to practice finding the materials that would be useful in locating information. Search and Find can be made into a booklet, individual worksheets, or a learning center.

## *JUST FOR YOU ACTIVITY*

OBJECTIVES:

The student will:

1.  Construct a picture based on ideas from a narrative.

2.  Construct a model book including front, back, cover, author, title, publisher, and copyright date.

GRADE LEVEL: Kindergarten or first

MATERIALS NEEDED:

Paper

Ditto to duplicate resource sheet

Resource sheet (see fig. 8.1)

Book: *Just for You* by Mercer Mayer

Pencils and crayons

Acetate for cover (optional)

Heavy duty stapler and staples

Additional assistance from an aide, older student, parent, or senior citizen to write what the students dictate

PROCEDURE:

This activity was designed to be used with a whole class. The students will make a class book for their teacher. This could be done for a special occasion such as American Education Week, Mother's Day, Father's Day, or the end of the year.

### *Preparation for Reading*

The library media specialist should ask students what they have done to help at home. After a few students have given their experiences, ask the students if anything went wrong when they have tried to help. Then have a few students relate their experiences.

### *Setting the Purpose for Listening*

The library media specialist can tell the students that they are going to hear a story about a little creature who tries to do nice things for his mother. Students should be instructed to listen to find out what ways the little creature tries to help his mother.

### *Reading/Listening Activity*

Before reading, the title and author/illustrator should be told. Read *Just for You* by Mercer Mayer.

Name: _____

Fig. 8.1. Resource sheet for *Just for You* activity.

*Follow-up Activities*

1. Have students relate what the creature tried to do to help his mother.

2. Students make a class book.

    A. Tell students that they will make a class book for their teacher. Point out that their book will have a front, back, cover, and title page. Also point out that the title page will have a title, author, publisher, and copyright date.

    B. Have students relate ways they help their teacher.

    C. Give students directions that they are to draw a picture of how they help their teacher. While they are drawing, they need to think about what they want to tell about their picture. Tell them someone will come to them and write down what they want to say.

    D. Have students do the drawings.

    E. Take dictation and have students write their names.

    F. Collect papers.

    G. Put papers together.

    1) Acetate sheet on outside for cover
    2) Blank sheet
    3) Title page with
        a) Title: *Just for You*
        b) Author(s)
        c) Publisher—School name plus "Publishing Company" (for example, Rosemont Elementary School would be "Rosemont Publishing Company"
    4) Copyright date
    5) Text (students' work)
    6) Blank sheet
    7) Acetate sheet

    H. Students can then present teacher with finished book.

ASSESSMENT:

1. Did the students construct a picture based on an idea from the story?

2. Did the students construct a model book including front, back, cover, author, title, publisher, and copyright date?

## *STUDENT-MADE CARD CATALOG*

OBJECTIVES:

The student will:

1.  Make a simplified author card for the class card catalog.

2.  Be able to place his or her card behind appropriate letter of the alphabet for his or her author card.

GRADE LEVEL: First or second

·MATERIALS NEEDED:

Sheets of medium weight paper that are 8½" x 11" (see fig. 8.2, Blank resource sheet, page 90)

Ditto to duplicate resource sheet on paper

Overhead transparency of resource sheet

Overhead projector

Box to hold 8½" x 11" sheets

Guide cards with all alphabet letters

Pencils and crayons

Pen for writing on transparency

Additional assistance from older students, parents, or senior citizens (optional, but helpful to pass out materials prior to students' arrival and to take dictation from less able students)

PREVIOUS LEARNING EXPECTATIONS:

Students must be able to:

1.  Locate author's name, the title, and the call number on a book.

2.  Transfer letters/words from book to paper.

3.  Recognize or match alphabet letters.

4.  Explain how easy books are organized.

5.  Explain how the call number of easy books is determined.

PROCEDURE:

This activity is designed to be used with a classroom or group of students during at least three class periods. Modifications to extend or shorten this time frame may be needed. In lessons prior to this activity, the students should have been able to find the author, title, and call number on an easy book. Students need an opportunity to find a book that they have enjoyed. The library media specialist can select a short easy book that is a favorite. After reading the book, the library media specialist should review (1) where author, title, and call number are located on their book (students can demonstrate where each is located by pointing to it when directed and be corrected if needed;

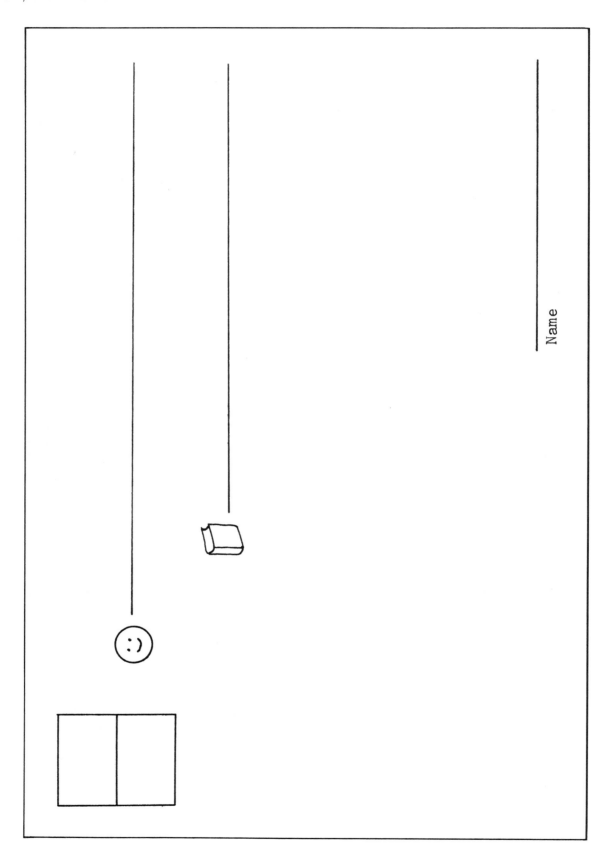

Fig. 8.2. Resource sheet for Student-made Card Catalog.

older students, parents or senior citizens may be useful to assist in passing out materials and guiding students), (2) how the call number is determined, and (3) how the easy books are organized.

Briefly explain that the card catalog is an index that helps older students find all kinds of materials in the library media center. Explain that they will be making a class card catalog so they can locate favorite books in the easy collection and that it will help them when they are older to use the other card catalog.

Then, using the overhead transparency, the library media specialist will have students help her fill out the author card for the book that was read. Students will then be directed to fill in author, title, and call number on their own card. You may wish to pair a nonreader with an able reader to work as a team. As students are finished, collect papers for the next class.

During the next class, the library media specialist would want to review the previous lesson. Additionally, the library media specialist should explain the organization of the other card catalog and that their class card catalog will also be organized in alphabetical order. The students should illustrate some part of the book on their author card. When they have finished, they should be assisted to file the author card behind the appropriate letter.

During the next class, the library media specialist needs to review the organization of the easy collections and relate the call number to the location of easy books. Then, students could tell classmates about their author card and show them where the book would be located.

ASSESSMENT:

(This assessment would not apply to students who speak another language.)

1.  Did each student make a simplified author card?

2.  Was the student able to place his or her card behind the appropriate letter of the alphabet for his or her author?

## EZRA JACK KEATS CENTER

OBJECTIVES:

The student will:

1. Become familiar with the works of Ezra Jack Keats.

2. Enjoy literature.

3. Do activities following the viewing of or listening to Ezra Jack Keats' books.

GRADE LEVEL: First

MATERIALS NEEDED:

Books by Ezra Jack Keats: *HI, CAT!*
*Jennie's Hat*
*A Letter to Amy*
*Louie*
*Over in the Meadow*
*Pet Show!*

Film: *Ezra Jack Keats* (Weston Woods, 1971)

Sound filmstrips: *Whistle for Willie* (Weston Woods)
*The Snowy Day* (Weston Woods)

Worksheets

16-mm projector

Sound filmstrip projector or a sound filmstrip previewer (or a filmstrip projector and cassette tape recorder)

Pencils

Crayons

PROCEDURE:

This activity is designed to be used with individuals, small groups, or a whole class. Students can work through the learning center (fig. 8.3) individually at their own pace or the classroom teacher or the library media specialist could use the worksheets after each activity.

If the materials for these activities are not available, substitutions could be made. Other activities could be developed to expand these materials.

This learning center has five numbered activities and a quest activity. The directions for the numbered activities can be typed on a primary typewriter. The directions for the numbered activities are as follows:

(Text continues on page 101.)

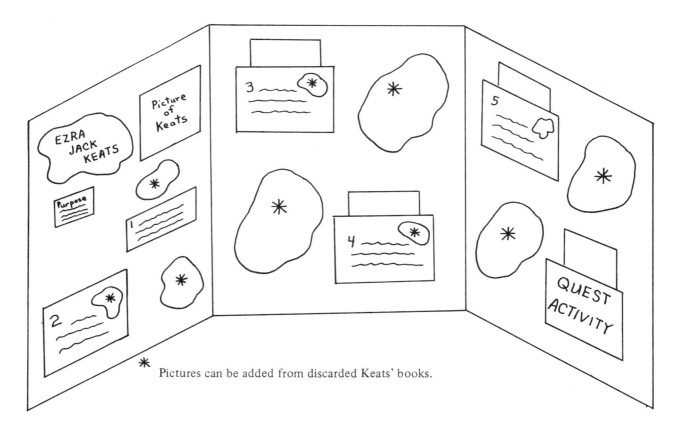

* Pictures can be added from discarded Keats' books.

Fig. 8.3. Suggested layout for the Ezra Jack Keats Center. See following pages for description of numbered activities.

# 1

Watch and Listen
   Watch the film *Ezra Jack Keats*.
   Watch the sound filmstrips:
      *Whistle for Willie*
      *The Snowy Day*

# 2

Listen and Do
   Listen to the story *Over in the
      Meadow*.
   Complete the dot-to-dot that is
      in the pocket. (See figure 8.4 on page 97.)

# 3

Listen and Do
  Listen to the story *Jennie's Hat.*
  Design a hat for Jennie.  (See figure 8.5 on page 98.)

# 4

  Help Make a Book
    Read the book *Pet Show!*
    Draw a page for the class book.
      Include your real or imaginary
      pet and yourself in your draw-
      ing. Write a sentence or two
      about your picture. Then sign
      your name. (See figure 8.6 on page 99.)

# 5

Listen and Match
 Listen to the stories:
  *A Letter to Amy*
  *HI, CAT!*
  *Louie*
 Match the characters/items
  from Ezra Jack Keats' books.
 (See figure 8.7 on page 100.)

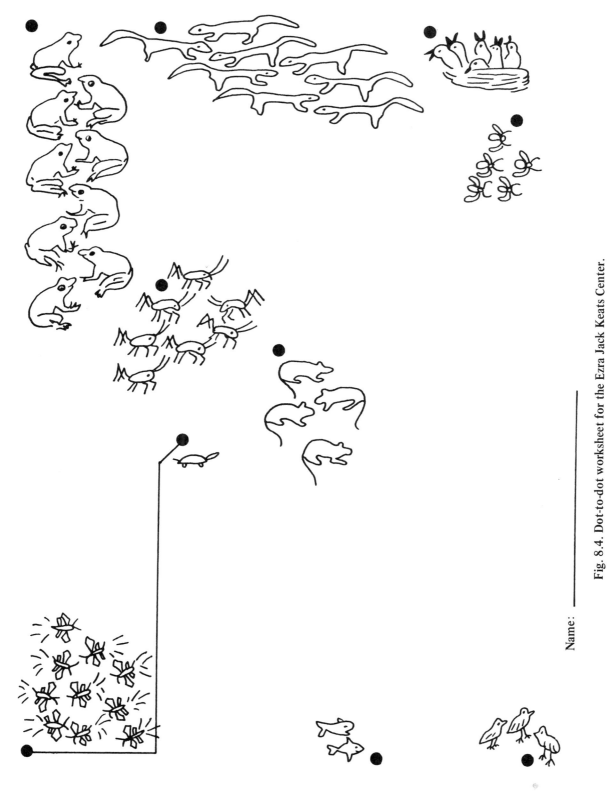

**Fig. 8.4. Dot-to-dot worksheet for the Ezra Jack Keats Center.**

Name: _____

Illustrations adapted from *OVER IN THE MEADOW* by Ezra Jack Keats. Copyright © 1971 by Ezra Jack Keats. Reprinted by permission of Four Winds Press, a division of Scholastic Inc., and the Ezra Jack Keats Foundation, 1005 East 4th Street, Brooklyn, NY 11230.

**Fig. 8.5. Design a hat worksheet for the Ezra Jack Keats Center.**

From *JENNIE'S HAT* by Ezra Jack Keats. Illustrations by the writer. Copyright © 1966 by Ezra Jack Keats. Reprinted by permission of Harper & Row, Publishers, Inc.

Fig. 8.6. Draw and write worksheet for the Ezra Jack Keats Center.

Name _____

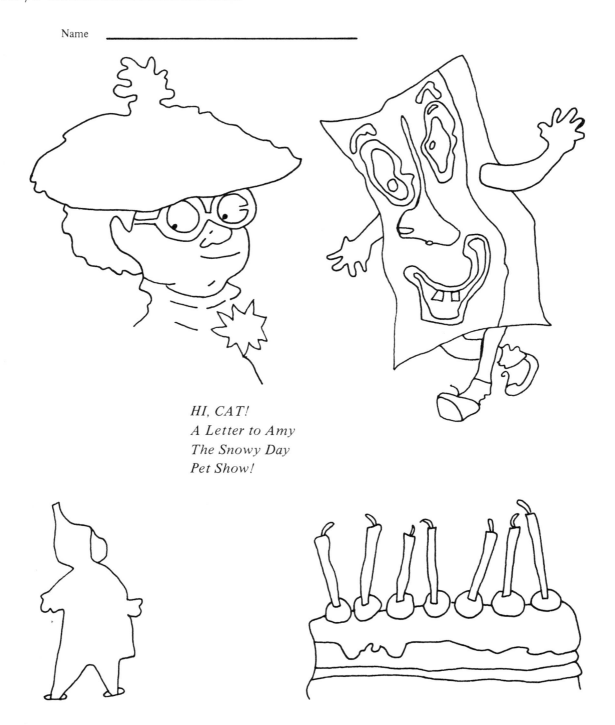

HI, CAT!
A Letter to Amy
The Snowy Day
Pet Show!

**Fig. 8.7. Match the characters worksheet for the Ezra Jack Keats Center.**

The quest activity is as follows:

*Quest Activity*

Directions: Write your answers on your own paper.

Use the *More Junior Authors* and *Newbery and Caldecott Medal Books: 1956-1965* to answer the following questions about Ezra Jack Keats.

1. When was Ezra Jack Keats born?

2. Where was he born?

3. Name the first book he wrote and illustrated.

4. Does our library media center own this book? Hint: Use the card catalog.

5. For which book did he win the Caldecott Medal?

6. How did his father feel about his becoming an artist?

7. Which of Ezra Jack Keats' books is your favorite?

8. Why do you think that book is your favorite?

9. If you had a chance to talk with Ezra Jack Keats, what would you ask him?

10. What would you like him to know about you?

*Anwers to Keats Center*

Quest Activity

1. 1916

2. Brooklyn, New York

3. *The Snowy Day*

4. Answers will vary. Question asked whether the library media center owned a copy of *The Snowy Day.*

5. *The Snowy Day*

6. His father disapproved.

7. Answers will vary. Question asked which book was student's favorite.

8. Answers will vary. Question asked why that was student's favorite book.

9. Answers will vary. Question asked what student would ask Ezra Jack Keats if he or she met him.

10. Answers will vary. Question asked students what he or she would like Ezra Jack Keats to know about himself or herself.

ASSESSMENT:

1.  Were the students able to tell the name of the author?

2.  Did the students enjoy the literature? (Students could use every pupil response to evaluate whether that selection should be used with another class.)

3.  Did the students do the activities?

## *ANIMAL DICTIONARY LAP PACK*

OBJECTIVES:

The student will:

1.  Be able to alphabetize words to the fourth letter.

2.  Use guide words to locate an entry word.

3.  Be able to interpret information in the dictionary entries of a beginning dictionary.

4.  Be able to find and use definitions that are given in a beginning dictionary.

5.  Be able to distinguish between several definitions.

6.  Be able to write the respellings of given words.

7.  Be able to write the syllables for given words.

8.  Be able to locate the correct spelling when given two choices.

9.  Be able to interpret information given in the illustrations in a beginning dictionary.

GRADE LEVEL:   Second or third

MATERIALS NEEDED:

Copy of Dictionary Lap Pack for each student

Macmillan's *Beginning Dictionary,* 1981 edition

Pencils

Paper

Filmstrip: "What's in the Dictionary?" *Using the Elementary School Library.* SVE, 1968. An introductory filmstrip that includes such topics as entry words, guide words, interpreting entries, definitions, pronunciation, syllabication, and interpreting illustrations could be substituted.

Alphabet strips (if needed)

Slips used to monitor student progress (optional)

PROCEDURE:

This activity is designed to be used with individuals, small groups, or a whole class. Students could work through this lap pack individually at their own pace or the library media specialist (or classroom teacher) could use these as individual lessons. The student's work should be checked after each activity. The use of student progress slips would be beneficial for record keeping if students are working at their own pace.

ASSESSMENT:

Were the students able to complete these activities and get all answers correct? The expectation is that students will be able to get *all* answers correct.

## *Dictionary Lap Pack*

Directions: Read and follow *all* directions as you come to them. Write all answers on your own paper. For this lap pack, you will use Macmillan's *Beginning Dictionary* 1981 edition.

NOTE: If you need help, please ask for assistance!!

View the filmstrip "What's in the Dictionary?"

### Activity 1

In the dictionary, the words that are defined are called entry words. They are usually in bold dark print. The entry words are in alphabetical order. Put the following animals in alphabetical order.

| | |
|---|---|
| llama | cougar |
| mink | rabbit |
| hedgehog | eagle |
| tortoise | wren |
| scallop | iguana |

### Activity 2

When using a dictionary, it wouldn't make sense to look for the word *animal* at the end of the dictionary, just as it wouldn't make sense to look for the word *zebra* at the beginning of the dictionary. Try to think of the dictionary as being divided into three sections: the beginning having words that start with the letters A-G, the middle having words that start with the letters H-P, and the end having words that start with the letters Q-Z.

| Beginning A-G | Middle H-P | End Q-Z |
|---|---|---|

Which part of the dictionary will you find the following animals? Only do the starred * items if told to do them. Write *B* for beginning, *M* for middle and *E* for end.

| | | | |
|---|---|---|---|
| 1. | jaguar | * 9. | wasp |
| 2. | falcon | *10. | sloth |
| 3. | dromedary | *11. | puffin |
| 4. | yak | *12. | bobolink |
| 5. | canary | *13. | pheasant |
| 6. | grizzly bear | *14. | octopus |
| 7. | trout | *15. | zebra |
| 8. | llama | *16. | mole |

**Activity 3**

When you look up words in the dictionary, you need to be able to use the alphabet. In the dictionary, there are many words listed for each letter of the alphabet. Keep in mind that the first letter of the word tells you in what section of the dictionary to start looking. If the first letter of the words are the same, you have to look at the second letter to find words. For example: The words *rooster* and *ram* start with the letter *r*. In the dictionary the word *ram* would come first because the second letter, *a,* in *ram* comes before the second letter, *o,* in *rooster.*

Part 1

Put the following words in alphabetical order:

1. pig
2. perch
3. pheasant
4. parrot
5. poodle

Part 2

When words have the same first two letters, you need to go to the third letter to decide which word goes first. For example: With the words *sheep* and *shark*, the word *shark* would come first because the third letter, *a,* in *shark* comes before the third letter, *e,* in *sheep.* Put the following words in alphabetical order:

6. dog
7. doe
8. dodo
9. donkey
10. dolphin

Part 3

If the first three letters of the words are exactly the same, you need to look at the fourth letter of each word. For example: If you are working with the words *skid* and *skin,* the word *skid* would come first because the fourth letter, *d,* in *skid* comes before the fourth letter, *n,* in *skin.* Put the following words in alphabetical order:

11. meat
12. meadow
13. meal
14. meant
15. measles

## Activity 4

To find words quickly in the dictionary use *guide words.* Guide words in *most* dictionaries are found at the top of the page. In Macmillan's *Beginning Dictionary,* 1981 edition, look on page 194. Look at the top left hand corner. Find *dolphin/doom.* They are the guide words. Notice that *dolphin* is the first entry word on that page and *doom* is the last entry on that page. Words that are in that dictionary and come alphabetically between those guide words will be found on that page. Write the guide words that are found on the following pages:

1.  page 155
2.  page 358
3.  page 618
4.  page 215
5.  page 96

## Activity 5

When you want to find a word in the dictionary, you need to decide if that word comes alphabetically between the two guide words on the page on which you are looking. Put the words that follow under the correct guide words:

| | | | |
|---|---|---|---|
| 1.  file | 3.  fiddle | 5.  figure | 7.  fez |
| 2.  fig | 4.  field | 6.  fighter | 8.  fierce |

```
  few/fig
  page 240
```

```
  fight/filings
  page 241
```

## Activity 6

Find the entry words that follow in Macmillan's *Beginning Dictionary,* 1981 edition. Write the guide words that are on the page where you find each word.

Example: herring (found on page 303) *hence/he's*

1.  salmon
2.  elk
3.  leopard
4.  wolf
5.  starling
6.  alpaca

Illustrations used with permission of Volk Art, Inc., Pleasantville, NJ 08232.

**Activity 7**

*Reminder:* Entry words are in bold dark print so they will be easier to find.

Find the following animals using the dictionary. Tell whether the animal usually flies, swims, or walks.

| | | | |
|---|---|---|---|
| 1. | gnu | 6. | boar |
| 2. | killdeer | 7. | pickerel |
| 3. | guppy | 8. | sturgeon |
| 4. | aphid | 9. | rhea |
| 5. | gibbon | | |

**Activity 8**

The words next to each number below are guide words. Then there are four words below each set of guide words. Write the words from each set that would come between the guide words. After you are finished, you can check your own work by finding the guide words in the dictionary.

1. rhea/rich
   
   retriever          rhinoceros          rhea          roach

2. ground/grub
   
   grouse             gull                groundhog     greyhound

3. chess/chili
   
   chihuahua          chickadee           cheetah       chipmunk

4. dolphin/doom
   
   dormouse           dodo                donkey        dolphin

5. ghetto/giraffe
   
   gibbon             goat                gnu           giraffe

6. picturesque/pile[1]
   
   pinto              pigeon              pickerel      pike

7. suspension bridge/sweat
   
   swan               swordfish           swallow       swift

8. jackknife/Japanese
   
   jackal             jay                 jaguar        jack rabbit

9. pueblo/pump
   
   puffin             puma                pupa          pup

10. Saint Bernard/salt
    
    salmon             sandpiper           sardine       salamander

**Activity 9**

Find page P3 in the back of the dictionary. This page shows you where each part of the entry is located. Use page P3 as a guide. At the same time, turn to page 406 to answer the following questions.

1. What are the guide words?

2. What is the first entry word listed?

3. How many entry words are on this page?

4. Write the two acceptable pronunciations for "mongrel."

5. Look in the *language note* on Montana. Why should Montana not have been given that name?

6. What kinds of animals would a mongoose kill?

7. Write the definition for mongrel.

8. Look at the second definition for monstrous. Write the example sentence.

9. What is the plural of mongoose? (NOTE: plural means more than one.)

10. What entry words are illustrated?

**Activity 10**

Look up the entry words in the word box. Find the definition below that best fits each entry word. Write that word beside the correct number of its definition.

| WORD BOX | | | |
|---|---|---|---|
| gopher | cuckoo | puffin | porpoise |
| hedgehog | owl | oyster | salmon |

1. Is an intelligent (smart) animal.

2. Is a sea bird.

3. Hunts for food at night.

4. Lays eggs in fresh water.

5. Builds long tunnels.

6. Has a soft body and hinged shell.

7. Lays its eggs in other birds' nests.

8. Can roll up in a ball.

**Activity 11**

In some dictionaries, entry words that have the same spelling, but different meanings, have a number after them. Use the dictionary to fill in the blanks in the sentences below.

NOTE: Be sure to include the number!!

1. The _____ is a bird with a sharp beak. (hawk$^1$  hawk$^2$ )

2. The _____ is a small animal that lives underground. (mole$^1$  mole$^2$ )

3. The _____ is a relative of the shark. (skate$^1$  skate$^2$ )

4. The black _____ makes a harsh cry. (crow$^1$  crow$^2$ )

5. _____ is fish eggs. (roe$^1$  roe$^2$ )

6. The _____ has flippers and lives mostly in cold water. (seal$^1$  seal$^2$ )

7. The white _____ is a symbol of peace. (dove$^1$  dove$^2$ )

8. _____ is a good tasting flatfish. (sole$^1$  sole$^2$  sole$^3$ )

9. The _____ is a reddish-brown deer. (roe$^1$  roe$^2$ )

**Activity 12**

A word can have more than one meaning. In the dictionary, each definition (meaning) is numbered. Look up the words that are underlined in each sentence. Write the number of the definition that fits the word as it is used in that sentence.

1. There is not a <u>tooth</u> in the turtle's mouth.

2. Did your dog <u>stray</u> from home?

3. Did the squirrel <u>store</u> food in the tree for winter?

4. The bird's <u>wing</u> was hurt.

5. The cat has <u>whisker(s)</u> on its face.

6. The <u>salmon</u> swims up the river to lay its eggs.

7. The bear sleeps in its <u>den</u> in the winter.

**Activity 13**

The dictionary helps you to pronounce (say) words correctly. Sometimes when you see a word, you may not know that word. If you could hear that word, you might know it. Use the dictionary and write the pronunciation (the way the word sounds) for the following words. You may need to look at page P3 to remember where the pronunciation is.

Example: leopard (lep′ərd)

1. cougar
2. wren
3. vulture
4. chihuahua

5. jackal
6. crow
7. weasel
8. ewe

**Activity 14**

Some words have more than one correct pronunciation. Find each of the words below in the dictionary and write the two acceptable ways to say them.

Example: cuckoo (ko̅o̅′ ko̅o̅ or kook′ o̅o̅)

1. walrus
2. aphid
3. scallop
4. falcon

5. ocelot
6. fillet
7. donkey
8. bison

**Activity 15**

The dictionary also shows you where to divide words into syllables. In this dictionary, the division into syllables comes just before the pronunciation. Find the word *marsupial*. Just before the pronunciation, you will see "mar · su · pi · al." The dots separate the word into syllables. Using the dictionary, divide the words below into syllables.

1. beaver
2. eagle
3. sturgeon
4. dromedary
5. copperhead

6. octopus
7. jaguar
8. buzzard
9. whippoorwill

**Activity 16**

The dictionary can help you to spell words correctly. If you don't know how to spell a word, write down several guesses on a piece of paper. Then look up your guesses. Many times you will be able to find the word by looking up your guesses. If you don't find it, look before and after where you think the word should be. If you still have not found it, try to think of other ways the sounds of that word might be spelled. Look up the pair of words in the sentences below. Choose the one that is spelled correctly.

1. The (grayhound  greyhound) is a slender dog that runs very fast.

2. My father caught a (carp  karp) at the lake.

3. (Barracuda  Baracuda) is a fierce fish that lives in warm water.

4. The (armmadilo  armadillo) digs in the ground for insects to eat.

5. The (chetah  cheetah) is from the cat family and lives in Africa and Asia.

6. I caught a ten pound (bass  bas) with my new fishing pole.

**Activity 17**

The pictures in the dictionary can help you understand more about the entry word. Find the underlined word in each sentence. Look at the picture for that entry word to answer the questions.

1. How many arms does an <u>octopus</u> have?

2. What does a <u>water buffalo</u> have on its head?

3. Does a <u>beaver</u> have a long tail, a skinny tail, a flat tail, or no tail?

4. Does a <u>teal</u> live in a desert?

5. Where does a <u>mole</u> live?

6. What color is a <u>cardinal</u>?

7. Does a <u>yak</u> have long hair, short hair, or no hair?

8. Is a <u>llama</u> more like a fish, a bird, or camel?

CONGRATULATIONS!

## *Answer Sheet*

### Activity 1

| | | | | |
|---|---|---|---|---|
| 1. | cougar | 6. | mink |
| 2. | eagle | 7. | rabbit |
| 3. | hedgehog | 8. | scallop |
| 4. | iguana | 9. | tortoise |
| 5. | llama | 10. | wren |

### Activity 2

| | | | | |
|---|---|---|---|---|
| 1. | M | * 9. | E |
| 2. | B | *10. | E |
| 3. | B | *11. | M |
| 4. | E | *12. | B |
| 5. | B | *13. | M |
| 6. | B | *14. | M |
| 7. | E | *15. | E |
| 8. | M | *16. | M |

### Activity 3

| Part 1 | | Part 2 | | Part 3 | |
|---|---|---|---|---|---|
| 1. | parrot | 6. | dodo | 11. | meadow |
| 2. | perch | 7. | doe | 12. | meal |
| 3. | pheasant | 8. | dog | 13. | meant |
| 4. | pig | 9. | dolphin | 14. | measles |
| 5. | poodle | 10. | donkey | 15. | meat |

### Activity 4

| | |
|---|---|
| 1. | crest/crisp |
| 2. | lantern/lash |
| 3. | stool/storm |
| 4. | emu/end |
| 5. | came/campus |

**Activity 5**

few/fig                          fight/filings

fig                              file

fiddle                           figure

field                            fighter

fez

fierce

**Activity 6**

1. Saint Bernard/salt
2. eliminate/embargo
3. legislative/leopard
4. wives/wood
5. starboard/state
6. aloud/aluminum

**Activity 7**

1. walks                         6. walks
2. flies                         7. swims
3. swims                         8. swims
4. flies                         9. walks (This bird does not fly.)
5. walks

**Activity 8**

1. rhinoceros, rhea              6. pigeon, pike
2. grouse, groundhog             7. swan, swallow
3. chihuahua, chickadee          8. jaguar, jack rabbit
4. donkey, dolphin               9. puffin, puma
5. gibbon, giraffe              10. salmon, salamander

## Activity 9

1. money/monthly
2. money
3. 16
4. (mung grəl and mong grəl)
5. In student's own words: There are few mountains in Montana.
6. snakes
7. A dog or other animal that is a mixture of breeds.
8. "The little girl thought the elephant she saw at the zoo was a monstrous animal."
9. mongooses
10. mongoose and monkey

## Activity 10

1. porpoise
2. puffin
3. owl
4. salmon
5. gopher
6. oyster
7. cuckoo
8. hedgehog

## Activity 11

1. hawk[1]
2. mole[2]
3. skate[2]
4. crow[2]
5. roe[1]
6. seal[1]
7. dove[1]
8. sole[3]
9. roe[2]

## Activity 12

1. #1
2. #1
3. #2
4. #1
5. #2
6. #1
7. #1

## Activity 13

1. (ko͞o´gər)
2. (ren)
3. (vul´chər)
4. (chi wä wə)
5. (jak´əl)
6. (krō)
7. (wē´zəl)
8. (yo͞o)

### Activity 14

1. (wôl´ rəs or wol´ rəs)
2. (ā´ fid or af´ id)
3. (skol´ əp or skal´ əp)
4. (fôl´ kən or fal´ kən)
5. (os´ ə lot´ or ō´ sə lot´)
6. (fi lā´ or fil´ ā)
7. (dong´ kē or dung´ kē)
8. (bī´ sən or bī´ zən)

### Activity 15

1. bea · ver
2. ea · gle
3. stur · geon
4. drom · e · dar · y
5. cop · per · head
6. oc · to · pus
7. jag · uar
8. buz · zard
9. whip · poor · will

### Activity 16

1. greyhound
2. carp
3. barracuda
4. armadillo
5. cheetah
6. bass

### Activity 17

1. eight
2. long horns
3. a flat tail
4. no
5. underground
6. red
7. long hair
8. camel

## *SPAIN: USING AN ENCYCLOPEDIA*

OBJECTIVES:

The student will:

1. Identify and locate dictionaries.

2. Identify and locate encyclopedias.

3. Identify on print material the index.

4. Locate specific information in an index.

5. Locate information using
    A.  Alphabetical order by the fourth letter of word.
    B.  Visuals:
        1)  Photographs.
        2)  Captions.
        3)  Maps.
        4)  Graphs/charts.
    C.  Dictionaries.
    D.  Guide words.
    E.  Indexes.
    F.  Encyclopedias.

6. Locate a specific entry word in an intermediate dictionary.

7. Locate within an entry word in an intermediate dictionary:
    A.  Entry word.
    B.  Definition.

8. Locate the index of an encyclopedia.

9. Locate entry word(s) in the index.

10. Locate specific volume(s) by using letters or numbers on spine.

11. Locate article(s) in a volume by using guide words.

12. Select a dictionary to find word meaning.

13. Select an encyclopedia to locate specific information.

14. Use visuals to get information.

15. Use index to locate information.

16. Use guide words.

17. Use a dictionary to interpret information within entries by identifying entry word.

18. Use a dictionary to interpret information within entries by identifying definition.

19. Use a dictionary to select appropriate meaning for a given word.

20. Interpret simple maps.

21. Interpret simple charts.

22. Locate information in an encyclopedia:
    A. Interpret information in the index to locate specific articles.
    B. Use headings and subheadings.
    C. Use visuals within an article to get information.
    D. Skim to find a word or name, phrases, or date.

GRADE LEVEL: Third

MATERIALS NEEDED:

Copies of each worksheet for student

*The New Book of Knowledge,* 1982 edition

Pencils

Paper

Slips used to monitor student's progress (optional)

CURRICULUM CORRELATION:

This library media skills unit is designed to be used with the third-grade social studies unit on "Communities of the World." If other communities are studied, it can serve as a model to create materials for other communities or countries. These materials also provide some opportunity to practice map reading.

PROCEDURE:

This activity is designed to be used with individuals or small groups of students. Since these materials basically use two volumes, multiple copies of those volumes would be helpful. If a small group is working on these materials, starting times would need to be staggered. This activity could be used in lieu of traditional language arts activities with students taking turns. For example: During an hour and a half time period, six students could use these materials for fifteen minutes. Before using these materials, a film or filmstrip to introduce or review use of an encyclopedia would be helpful. Students are expected to work through these materials (whether they are made into a booklet, individual worksheets, or a learning center) from the beginning. Students work through these materials at their own pace supervised by either the library media specialist or the classroom teacher. The student's work should be checked after each activity. The use of student progress slips would be beneficial for record keeping if students are working at their own pace. If these materials are used with a different edition of *The New Book of Knowledge,* you would need to check to see all activities and answers still apply. If this unit is made into a learning center, a travel agent may be able to provide some colorful pictures of Spain that could be used to make the center attractive.

ASSESSMENT:

Were the students able to answer the questions on the activity sheets? Students are expected to be able to obtain the correct answers with or without assistance.

*Spain: Using an Encyclopedia*

PURPOSE:

By working through this unit on Spain, you will:

I. Decide what the key words are before looking for information.

II. Find information in an encyclopedia by
    A. using the index.
    B. using guide words.
    C. using main headings and subheadings.
    D. using captions, charts, maps, and photographs.

DIRECTIONS:

1. Use the 1982 *The New Book of Knowledge* to answer the questions.

2. Write your name on all of your papers.

3. Do not write on these materials unless you are told to write on them.

4. Get your answers checked after every activity.

5. If you need help, please ask for assistance.

### The Key Word

When you have an assignment, you first need to know which words or names you will look up in the encyclopedia. Read the sentences below. What is the key word you would search for in the encyclopedia?

Example: What is the capital? The key word is *capital.*

1. What foods do the people grow?

2. Do the people have to pay for their education?

3. What is the largest city?

4. What is the name of the mountain range?

5. What do the people do for recreation?

6. What colors are the flag?

7. What language do most of the people speak?

8. What are the names of dances that the people do?

**The Index**

The index makes the job of finding information easier and quicker. The index is arranged in alphabetical order. The main words in the index are called entry words just like in the dictionary. In some encyclopedias, there is one index in the last volume. Other encyclopedias also have an index in every book. Using the 1982 edition of *The New Book of Knowledge*, get volume 21. This is the main index. Turn to page 279. Find the entry *Madrid.*

Sample from an index

|  | Volume | Page number |
|---|---|---|
| Entry: Madrid |  |  |
| Subentries: Apollo tracking antenna | S | 340g |
| at mid-19th century, picture | S | 370 |
| bullfighting, picture | E | 304 |

Remember when you look up the name of a person, look up the last name. Use the index to answer which volume *and* page you will find:

1.  Francisco Franco (a person)

2.  bullfighting (in Mexico—use subentries)

3.  Valencia (city)

4.  Basque (language)

5.  Iberian peninsula

Look up the entry *Spain* in the index. Use the subentries to find the volume and page for:

6.  Picture of grape harvest

7.  Olive production

8.  Canary Islands

9.  Pictures of traditional costumes

The index sometimes tells you to look up other entries. After an entry or subentry, you may find the word *See*. When you look up the subentry *art* under *Spain*, which word(s) does it tell you to find?

Example: art  see Spanish art

What word(s) would you look up for:

10.  music

11.  architecture

12.  language

**Guide Words**

There are guide words in encyclopedias. They help you find entries quickly just like in the dictionary. While guide words are found at the top of many encyclopedias, they are found at the bottom in *The New Book of Knowledge*. (If there is a picture, map, or chart in the lower left or right hand corner, you will not find any guide words on that page.)

Answer the following questions using the 1982 *The New Book of Knowledge*.

1.   How many volumes are there?

2.   In which volume is the main index?

3.   Does each volume have an index?

4.   In which volume is the article "Spain"? Write the number and letter of the volume.

5.   On which page does the article "Spain" start?

6.   What are the guide words on pages 374 and 375 in volume 17/S?

**Main Headings and Subheadings**

Main headings and subheadings are aids within each article to help find information without reading the whole article. If you wanted to know what food grew in Spain, you would not need to read the whole article. You would look at the main headings and subheadings to find the answer. The subheading *Agriculture* would be where you would probably find the answer.

*Main headings* in *The New Book of Knowledge* have an arrow and all boldfaced capital letters. Main headings divide the article into sections.

*Subheadings* in *The New Book of Knowledge* are boldfaced and only the first letter of each important word is capitalized. Subheadings divide main headings into sections.

Turn to page 350 in volume 17/S in *The New Book of Knowledge*. The word *SPAIN* in the blue stripe is the name of the article. Find ►*THE PEOPLE*. That is the first main heading. Turn until you find the words *Language and Religion* in boldfaced lettering. That is the first subheading under the main heading ►*THE PEOPLE*.

*Skim* the main headings and subheadings when you are looking for information.

Use the article "Spanish Art and Architecture" that begins on page 360 in volume 17/S to answer the question below.

1.   What are the first three main headings?

Use the article "Spain" to answer the question below.

2.   What two subheadings are under the main heading ►*THE ECONOMY*?

**Spain**

Use the article "Spain" to answer the questions below. Also tell under which main heading or subheading you found the answer.

Example: Who were the last people to invade Spain?

Answer: The Moors / ►HISTORY AND GOVERNMENT

1. Spain has a climate much like a state in the United States. What is the state?

2. How many acres are most of the farms in Spain?

3. What is the largest city in Spain?

4. What is the most popular sport in Spain?

5. What is the religion of most of the Spanish people?

6. How high in feet and meters are the highest mountains (loftiest peaks)?

**Captions, Charts, Maps, and Photographs**

Much information can be learned from looking at the visuals (graphs, charts, photographs, and maps). There are usually captions (words that tell about the picture or photograph), keys, or bold lettering that give additional help in getting information.

Use the article "Spain" to answer the questions below.

1. Look at the photographs on pages 353, 354, and 358. Compare how the people of Spain dress with the way people in the United States dress.

2. Read the caption for the photograph on page 354. Who is the monument in honor of and what did the person do?

3. Find the map of Spain. Use the key. How do many people who live near Madrid earn money?

4. Find the city of Murcia on the east coast. What three things are important to that area for the people to earn money?

5. What ocean is west of Spain?

6. What country is north of Spain?

7. About how many miles is it from Madrid to France?

8. Read the caption for the photographs on page 353. On what do olives grow?

Turn to page 356. Find the box labeled *Facts and Figures*. This helps the reader find answers to questions that are often wanted. Use this box to answer the questions below.

9. What is the population of Spain?

10. What is the Spanish name for Spain?

11. What is their money (monetary unit) called?

12. Name three products the people of Spain export. Use a dictionary to tell what the word *export* means.

13. Look on page 368. What are the Spanish words for:

a. August          d. dog

b. eight           e. mother

c. Thursday      f. school

*Answer Sheet*
*Spain Unit*

### The Key Word

1. foods
2. education
3. city
4. mountain or mountain range
5. recreation
6. flag
7. languages
8. dances

### The Index

1. F 450
2. M 242
3. S 357
4. L 40
5. I 493
6. A 98
7. 0 101, 102
8. I 427-28
9. C 350 AND D 264
10. Spanish music
11. Spanish architecture
12. Spanish language

### Guide Words

1. 21
2. 21
3. Yes
4. 17/S
5. 350
6. Spain/Spanish-American War

### Main Headings and Subheadings

1. Painting
   Architecture
   Sculpture and Crafts
2. Industry
   Agriculture

### Spain

1. California/climate
2. 2½ acres/Agriculture
3. Madrid/ ► CITIES
4. Soccer/Recreation
5. Roman Catholic/Language and Religion
6. 11,000 feet, 3,350 meters/ ► THE LAND

**Captions, Charts, Maps, and Photographs**

1.  Answers will vary. The gist should be that the people of Spain dress much like the people of the United States.
2.  Cervantes. He wrote *Don Quixote.*
3.  industry
4.  olives, grapes, citrus fruits
5.  Atlantic
6.  France
7.  Approximately 250 miles
8.  trees
9.  36,700,000 people
10.  Estado Español
11.  peseta
12.  Any three of: manufactured goods, citrus fruits, olive oil, wine, fish, cork, tobacco. Definition of the word export.

    a.  agosto                    d.  perro
    b.  ocho                      e.  madre
    c.  jueves                    f.  escuela

## *NOVEL UNIT FOR CHARLOTTE'S WEB*

### *General Information*[1]

Students from the regular classroom and those identified as gifted and talented can profit from and enjoy novel/literature units. These units can be of a short duration (one or two sessions) or can be extended over a long period. The following novel unit was intended to be used over an extended period. A small group of students (ten to twelve students maximum) can come to the library media center every day or perhaps two or three times a week. *Response Guides for Teaching Children's Books* by Albert B. Somers and Janet Evans Worthington is an excellent source for additional ideas which can be used or extended.

OBJECTIVES:

The student will:

1. Read a novel of some duration.

2. State the plot.

3. State the characteristics of the three major figures.

4. Participate in interrelated arts activities.

5. Use a dictionary and contextual clues to discover word meaning.

GRADE LEVEL:

Third-grade gifted and talented students or

Third-grade students who are able readers

MATERIALS NEEDED:

Multiple copies of *Charlotte's Web* by E. B. White

Dictionaries (if needed)

Watercolor paper

Watercolor paints

Drawing paper

Crayons

Book or chart that shows parts of a spider

Copies of questions and vocabulary for students

PROCEDURE:

This novel unit is designed to be used with a small group of very able or gifted and talented third-grade students with direction from the library media specialist. Students are expected to be able to read *Charlotte's Web* independently and on their own time. Cooperation between the library media specialist, the classroom teacher, and the home is beneficial to the student. The classroom teacher may be able to lighten the student's workload while participating in the novel unit. A letter may be sent home to parents explaining what the students will be doing. Parents should be encouraged to set a family reading time in the evening to foster and encourage reading as a form of family recreation. Students usually will be expected to finish reading the chapters prior to arriving at the discussion group. During the first meeting the library media specialist should let students know that they will be reading a novel as a group and what will be expected of them. After doing the initiating activities, the library media specialist should reveal which novel is to be read. If students say they have read *Charlotte's Web* or seen the film, reassure them that that does not matter since they will be doing various activities with it and any good piece of literature can and should be enjoyed more than once. Provide each student with a copy of *Charlotte's Web* and a dictionary (if needed). Instruction on using the dictionary and how to use contextual clues may be needed. Cooperation and planning with the classroom teacher is essential. Both the library media specialist and the classroom teacher may be able to share this responsibility.

## SUGGESTIONS FOR RUNNING THE DISCUSSION GROUP

Rules for running the discussion group should be discussed by the whole group. The rules can be decided during the first meeting. Some guidelines for the instructor to keep in mind are

1.  Care should be taken that one individual or a small group of students does not monopolize the discussion.

2.  Students should be allowed to question other students' ideas.

3.  Students should not be allowed to attack other students' ideas.

4.  Students need to be able to support their ideas.

Rather than telling the students the guidelines or rules, help the students come up with their own ideas for guidelines. At the end of this first meeting, provide each student with a copy of the vocabulary and discussion questions for chapters one and two. Students should try to predict what is going to happen from reading the title of each chapter. Tell them to read the questions prior to reading and to note words that are unknown. Students need to be prepared to define the vocabulary words as they are used in the text. They may need to write the definitions.

The materials that follow are only a guide and serve as a model. If the objectives for the reading program are not met or if another element is to be focused upon, modifications are certainly in order. The following materials group some chapters together and divide the book into twelve sections rather than twenty-two chapters. Other divisions may be more desirable depending on the time constraints and the students. The interrelated arts activities can be done at regular meeting times in lieu of discussion group. If this plan is followed, at least eighteen meetings would be needed.

The library media specialist may want to design a test to check on students' learning. Tests are not included because the discussion group should reflect what the students are learning and have learned. This activity primarily uses the novel as a vehicle for extending vocabulary, understanding theme and characterization, and participating in interrelated arts activities.

## INITIATING ACTIVITIES

1.  Have students do an improvisation of the following scenerio: The child's pet has to be given away because its behavior has been causing family problems. The students may select the type of pet, the behavior that is undesirable, and the actions that occur. This activity could be done several times with various students taking on the different roles of family members and having them provide various problems and solutions.

2.  Students could make a "Friendships Are ..." handdrawn slide show. Each student could contribute a slide. Then they could provide dialog for an audio tape.

**FORMAT FOR DISCUSSION GROUPS**

The format for the following activities is only suggested and should be modified to meet a particular situation. The following five steps are the recommended procedures for each discussion.

1.    Do the interrelated arts activity. In some cases it may be appropriate to do this step last.

2.    Discuss the vocabulary finding the words and reading them in context.

3.    Discuss the questions.

4.    Give the students a copy of the vocabulary and discussion questions.

5.    Have students predict what will happen by looking at the title of the next chapter.

**CHAPTERS 1 AND 2**

Vocabulary:

| | |
|---|---|
| injustice—page 3 | blissful—page 7 |
| miserable—page 4 | appetite—page 7 |
| specimen—page 5 | enchanted—page 9 |

Phrases:

untimely death—page 4

early risers—page 5

Discussion Questions:

Chapter 1

1.    Why does Mr. Arable go out with his ax?

2.    How does Fern react when she finds out what her father plans to do? Could she have reacted any other way?

3.    What would you have done in that situation if you had been Fern?

Chapter 2

1.    How does Fern treat Wilbur like a human baby?

2.    When Wilbur starts to grow, why is he moved to another home?

**CHAPTERS 3 AND 4**

Vocabulary:

| | |
|---|---|
| grindstones—page 14 | eaves—page 25 |
| scythes—page 15 | goslings—page 28 |
| hullabaloo—page 22 | glutton—page 29 |
| captivity—page 22 | stealthily—page 30 |
| innocently—page 23 | cunning—page 30 |
| reconsider—page 23 | |

Phrases:

bucket of slops—page 19

wheat middlings—page 22

Activity:

As a group, brainstorm words that characterize pigs, spiders, and rats. (Record and save this list. Use it at the end of the story to see if the characters seem to fit the stereotyped images the students have of these particular animals.)

Discussion Questions:

Chapter 3

1. In what tone of voice do you think the goose said the last paragraph on page 17 that continues on page 18?

2. Wilbur is not happy in his new home or when he escapes. Why do you think he was not happy in either situation?

3. How did the other characters, Mr. and Mrs. Zuckerman, Lurvy, the sheep, the gander, and the cows, feel about Wilbur's escape?

4. Have you ever wanted and wanted something, but were disappointed when you finally got it? Be prepared to tell about your experience.

5. Why do you think that when any animal broke loose it was of "great interest to the others"? (page 19)

Chapter 4

1. What do you think Wilbur's exacting plans for his day tell you about his personality?

2. Do you see any discrepancy between the day Wilbur plans and what he declares he wants (last paragraph on page 27)?

3. What do you think of the seventh paragraph on page 28? How do you think Wilbur felt when he said that?

4. Why do you think the "new" character waited all day before talking to Wilbur?

**CHAPTERS 5, 6, AND 7**

Activity:

Paint a watercolor of the scene painted by the author in the first paragraph in chapter 6.

Vocabulary:

clashers—page 32

gleam—page 33

objectionable—page 35

near-sighted—page 37

inheritance—page 39

wits—page 40

innocent—page 40

swathes—page 42

jubilee—page 43

interlude—page 43

morals—page 46

conscience—page 46

compunctions—page 46

untenable—page 47

lair—page 47

anaesthetic—page 48

conspiracy—page 49

hysterics—page 51

Phrases:

milk of rodent kindness—page 46

Discussion Questions:

Chapter 5

1. Why does Wilbur dislike Charlotte when he first meets her?

2. Why wasn't Wilbur worried by the goose's words: "He doesn't even know what's going to happen to him around Christmastime; he has no idea that Mr. Zuckerman and Lurvy are plotting to kill him."[1]

Chapter 6

1. Why do you think the author included the first paragraph in chapter 6?

2. Look at page 45. What does the third line tell you about how the goose feels or thinks about herself?

3. Why do you think Charlotte was not offended at Templeton's wanting the rotten egg?

4. Why do you think that Charlotte and Wilbur had opposite opinions about Templeton's wanting the rotten egg? What do their different opinions tell you about those two characters?

Chapter 7

1. Why do you think the author chose to give this chapter the title "Bad News"?

2. Why did Wilbur change his mind about Charlotte's killing insects?

3. What bad news does the sheep give Wilbur?

4. What was Wilbur's reaction when the sheep told what happens to pigs in early winter?

5. Does it seem possible that a tiny spider can save a pig? Why or why not?

**CHAPTER 8**

Vocabulary:

vaguely—page 53

Students' Instructions and Discussion Questions:

1. Be prepared to read chapter 8 aloud. Different students will take the characters' parts. You will read the dialogue as if you were the character leaving out "asked Fern," "replied Fern," and "asked Mrs. Arable, gazing at her daughter with a queer worried look."[2] In other words, you will only read what is in quotes.

2. If you were Fern's mother would you be concerned about her when she relates what happened in the barnyard? Why or why not? How do you think you would have handled the situation if you were Fern's mother?

3. What argument might Fern give that animals can "talk"?

**CHAPTER 9**

Vocabulary:

truffles—page 61

Discussion Questions:

1. Why do you think Charlotte let Wilbur try making a web instead of just telling him he couldn't?

2. Why is it important for Wilbur to be able to spin a web?

3. Have you ever seen anyone act as foolishly as Wilbur did? You may want to share what happened as long as you don't mention names or embarrass anyone.

4. Do you think Wilbur was embarrassed when he cried? (page 61)

5. What did the author mean by "Swallows passed on silent wings ..."?[3]

6. Why do you think Wilbur kept delaying going to sleep?

7. How do you think Wilbur felt when Charlotte said she would "save him"?

Activity:

Draw a spider. Label its parts.

**CHAPTERS 10 AND 11**

Activity:

Have the students do an improvisation of the following scenerio: Lurvy and the Zuckermans discover Charlotte's newest web with the words "Christmas Ham"[4]

Discussion Questions:

Chapter 10

1. What does "naturally patient" mean?

2. Why do you think Charlotte didn't think people were as smart as bugs?

3. Does the evening have breath? (page 75)

4. What does "shadows lengthened" mean?

5. At the end of this chapter, do you think Charlotte had a definite plan of what she would do with the web?

Chapter 11

1. Why do you think Mr. Zuckerman thinks the pig is so special after seeing the "Some Pig" sign, while Mrs. Zuckerman thinks the spider is special?

2. How do the Zuckermans change their opinion of Wilbur?

3. Who do you think let the secret out?

4. Why do you think the author named all the different kinds of cars and trucks that came rather than just saying that their driveway was full of cars and trucks?

5. How did the web change life on the Zuckerman's farm?

**CHAPTERS 12 AND 13**

Vocabulary:

particle—page 89              radiant—page 99

destiny—page 90              dung—page 104

Discussion Questions:

Chapter 12

1.  Why do you think Charlotte called roll at the meeting of the animals?

2.  Do "People believe almost anything they see in print"?[5]

3.  Why do you think the author had Templeton play a part in the plan to save Wilbur?

4.  Rather than use Templeton, how could the author have provided Charlotte with ideas for the slogans?

Chapter 13

1.  Why do you think the author goes into such detail describing how Charlotte created the "terrific" web?

2.  Why do you think the author had Charlotte eat only a "small" bug after such a "difficult task"?

3.  Why do you think the author had Templeton's words from the dump not be suitable?

4.  Wilbur had said he wasn't a terrific pig. Why do you think he now feels "radiant"?

5.  Why do you think Wilbur is able to get Charlotte to tell two stories and sing a song even though she is tired?

**CHAPTERS 14 AND 15**

Vocabulary:

mercilessly—page 106              miraculous—page 110

sociable—page 107              incessant—page 110

Discussion Questions:

Chapter 14

1.  Why do you think the author had Fern support her story that Charlotte talks by saying "Charlotte never fibs"?[6]

2.  Why do you think the author had Fern's mother ask what else happened in the story after scolding her for inventing the wild tale?

3.  How does Mrs. Arable's tone change on page 106? Why do you think it changed?

4.  Why do you think Mrs. Arable is worried about Fern when it is Avery who gets poison ivy, gets stung by wasps and bees, and breaks things?

5.  Why did Mrs. Arable tell Dr. Dorian that she could crochet and knit?

Chapter 15

1. What was the mood of chapter 15? What was the feeling toward summer's ending?

2. Wilbur tried to be "some pig" when the web said "some pig," "terrific" when the web said "terrific," and "radiant" when the web said "radiant." Do you think people try to be what others think or say about them?

3. Why do you think Wilbur only had bad dreams at night?

4. How did Wilbur respond to Charlotte's telling him she may not be able to go to the fair?

**CHAPTERS 16 AND 17**

Discussion Questions:

Chapter 16

1. What preparations were made for going to the fair?

2. How was Templeton persuaded to go to the fair? Who persuaded him?

3. Why do you think the old sheep gave Wilbur the advice to struggle when being put in the crate?

4. How do you account for the large vocabulary that Templeton had when he told Wilbur to "watch what you're doing" when he gets in the crate?

5. Why do you think Avery acted like a pig?

6. Why do you think the author had the truck roll downhill with no one behind the wheel?

Chapter 17

1. Why do you think the author included the first paragraph in Chapter 17?

2. How were Mrs. Arable and Mrs. Zuckerman like many parents before they let their children enjoy the fair?

3. In the last paragraph on page 131, the author repeats the word *wonderful* again and again. Why do you think he did that rather than use other similar words?

4. Why do you think the author made "Uncle" have an unpleasant personality?

**CHAPTERS 18 AND 19**

Vocabulary:

acute—page 148

Discussion Questions:

Chapter 18

1. What mood does the author create when Charlotte says (in the second paragraph), "I shall be writing tonight for the last time"?[7]

2. Why do you think Templeton called Charlotte a schemer?

3. Does Wilbur have an idea of what is happening or going to happen to Charlotte?

Chapter 18 (cont'd)

4. At first Charlotte tells Wilbur that she's too tired to sing a song, and then she gives him a lengthy reply to his asking what she was doing. How do you account for that?

5. What does Charlotte call what she made? Why do you think she used that name?

6. Does the author let you know exactly what she made?

Chapter 19

1. Why do you think the author chose to start this chapter with a repeat of what Charlotte had said at the end of chapter 18?

2. Why do you think the author chose to use the word *humble* for the web?

3. What interests Fern most in this chapter? How do you know that?

4. What do you think is happening to Charlotte?

**CHAPTERS 20 AND 21**

Discussion Questions:

Chapter 20

1. Describe Mrs. Zuckerman's reaction and behavior just before Wilbur gets the special award. What does that tell you about her character?

2. Why do you think the author had Charlotte's "hour of triumph" occur when she heard words of praise for Wilbur rather than when she created the "magnum opus"?

3. Why do you think the author had Wilbur faint?

4. Why do you think the author made Templeton a hero in this chapter? How was Templeton a hero?

5. Why do you think the author had Wilbur win a special prize rather than the prize that "Uncle" won?

6. Why do you think the author ended this chapter with "slapstick" comedy?

Chapter 21

1. Why did Charlotte feel Wilbur's success was also her success?

2. Why do you think a tear came to Wilbur's eye when he remembered his first reaction to Charlotte?

3. In the next to last paragraph on page 164, Charlotte thought about her life. How did she feel about her life?

4. How does Templeton react to Wilbur's demand that he get Charlotte's egg sac? What does that action tell you about Wilbur's personality?

5. What were some of the ways Wilbur tried to get Templeton to get the egg sac?

6. Why do you think the author had Wilbur resort to bribing Templeton by allowing him first choice of Wilbur's food in order to get the egg sac?

**CHAPTER 22**

Vocabulary:

garrulous—page 183

Discussion Questions:

1. What qualities do you think the author thinks are important in a friend?

2. Why do you think the author had three of Charlotte's daughters stay in the barn?

3. What do you think the author's philosophy is about death?

4. Even most villains have some good qualities. What are Templeton's?

5. Do you think there is any significance to the names of Charlotte's daughters?

**SUMMARY ACTIVITIES**

The students will:

1. Make a list of at least five words that describe the personality and character of Wilbur, Charlotte, and Templeton.

2. Compare the words they wrote in number 1 with the characteristics they listed in the activity for chapters 3 and 4.

3. Write a summary of this story including the problem, the solution, and the action that takes place.

ASSESSMENT:

1. Did the students read the novel *Charlotte's Web*?

2. Were the students able to state the plot in a short summary?

3. Were the students able to list at least five words to describe the characteristics of Wilbur, Charlotte, and Templeton?

4. Did the students use a dictionary and contextual clues to discover word meaning?

5. Did the students participate in interrelated arts activities?

6. Did the students participate in discussions? A tally could be made to determine if the students did participate and to determine the distribution of the participation. For each session, the library media specialist could use a sheet of paper on which each student's name is listed. Then as students make contributions to the discussion, a mark could be made next to his or her name.

## NOTES

[1] E. B. White, *Charlotte's Web* (New York: Harper & Row, 1952), 40.

[2] White, *Charlotte's Web*, 52.

[3] White, *Charlotte's Web*, 62.

## NOTES (cont'd)

[4] Albert B. Somers and Janet Evans Worthington, *Response Guides for Teaching Children's Books* (Urbana, Ill.: National Council of Teachers of English, 1979), 59.

[5] White, *Charlotte's Web*, 89.

[6] White, *Charlotte's Web*, 106.

[7] White, *Charlotte's Web,* 138.

## BIBLIOGRAPHY

Somers, Albert B., and Janet Evans Worthington. *Response Guides for Teaching Children's Books.* Urbana, Ill.: National Council of Teachers of English, 1979.

*SEARCH AND FIND*

OBJECTIVES:

The student will:

1. Identify and locate
    A. Easy collection.
    B. Records.
    C. Charts.
    D. Filmstrips.
    E. Periodicals
    F. Nonfiction collection.
    G. Card catalog.
    H. Fiction collection.
    I. Vertical file.
    J. Almanacs.
    K. Atlases.
    L. Kits.

2. Identify on print or nonprint materials
    A. Cover.
    B. Spine.
    C. Title
    D. Call number.

3. Explain the arrangement of
    A. Easy collection.
    B. Fiction collection.
    C. Periodicals.
    D. Nonprint.
    E. Vertical file.

4. Locate by using call numbers
    A. Books from the easy collection.
    B. Fiction book.
    C. Nonfiction.
    D. Nonprint.

5. Locate information using
    A. Alphabetical order by fourth letter of word.
    B. Card catalog.

OBJECTIVES (cont'd)

    6. Find entries (in card catalog) by using guide letters and guide words to find entries.

    7. Identify parts of the catalog card

       A. Call number.

       B. Author.

       C. Title.

    8. Locate entries (in card catalog) by using alphabetizing rules.

    9. Identify media code on catalog card.

  10. Identify available material on a specified topic.

  11. Locate date of publication on cover of a periodical.

  12. Use card catalog to get information.

  13. Apply alphabetizing rules (in card catalog).

  14. Use call number to locate specific materials in library media center.

GRADE LEVEL: Third or fourth

MATERIALS NEEDED:

Copies of each activity for student

Pencils

Paper

Slips used to monitor students' progress (optional)

PREVIOUS LEARNING EXPECTATIONS:

Students need to be able to do most of the objectives before starting this activity. This activity was generally designed to have students practice and refine the retrieval skills.

CURRICULUM CORRELATION:

This activity is to prepare students to locate a variety of materials regardless of the subject area. Students are also expected to put numbers with decimals in ascending numerical order.

PROCEDURE:

This activity was designed to be used with individuals or small groups of students. Students are expected to work through these materials (whether they are made into a booklet, individual worksheets, or a learning center) from the beginning. Students can work through these materials at their own pace supervised by the library media specialist. The students' work should be checked after each activity. The use of student progress slips would be beneficial for record keeping if students are working at their own pace. These materials would need to be checked to assure that they apply to the individual school library media center.

ASSESSMENT:

Were the students able to complete each activity? Assistance can be provided, but students must be able to demonstrate competency.

*Search and Find*

PURPOSE:

To have students review use of the card catalog and the organization of materials in the library media center in order to locate specific materials.

DIRECTIONS:

Read all information and answer the questions on each worksheet.

PLEASE! Do not write on any of these materials. Write on your own paper.

**Organizational Patterns**

Knowing how the library media center is arranged is important so you can find books and materials you need. If library media centers did not have a system for organizing materials, it would be difficult, if not impossible, to find needed materials. In this exercise you will explain how some materials are arranged. You will need to go to where these materials are located to try to figure out how they are organized.

Explain how each of the following is organized:

1. Easy books.

2. Fiction books.

3. Nonfiction books

4. Periodicals

5. Vertical file

6. Kits

7. Filmstrips

8. Records

9. Charts

10. Biographies

11. Reference collection

**Card Catalog—The Keys to the Library Media Center**

The card catalog is a useful tool in helping you find needed materials. Much information can be found on the cards in the card catalog. Use any drawer in the card catalog to answer the questions below.

Can you find the following kinds of information on the cards in the card catalog? The questions do not have to be true for every material in the library media center. You are to say whether this type of information is available in the card catalog.

1. Who wrote the material?

2. Who did the illustrations?

3.  Who published the materials?

4.  When was the material published or produced?

5.  What is the copyright date?

6.  What is the title of the material?

7.  What is contained in the material?

8.  How long or how many pages is the material?

9.  Where are needed materials found?

10. How much did the material cost?

### Call Number—The Address of a Book or Material

In the upper left-hand corner of the cards in the card catalog, you will find the call number for materials. The call number tells you where the material is located.

Use the cards below to answer the following questions.

1.  Where would the item on card 1 be located?

2.  Where would the item on card 2 be located?

3.  Where would the item on card 3 be located?

4.  Where would the item on card 4 be located?

5.  Where would the item on card 5 be located?

6.  Should an easy book $\frac{E}{S}$ be before, after, or with a book by Ruth M. Tensen?

7.  What kind of material is the item on card 5?

8.  What kind of material is the item on card 4?

9.  What does the Z stand for that is part of the call number on card 3?

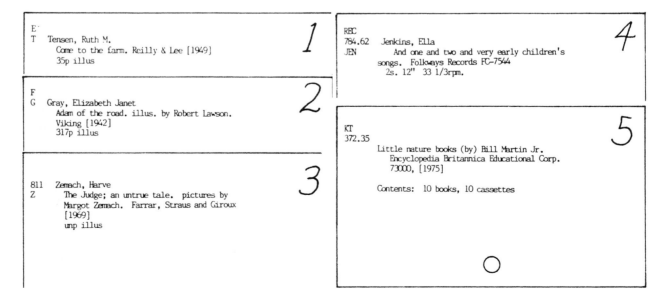

**The Dewey Decimal System**

All nonfiction books are arranged on the library media center shelves by the Dewey Decimal System—in numerical order. The Dewey number gives you two pieces of information: (1) where the material is and (2) what the subject of the material is.

## The Ten Dewey Decimal Categories

000-099   General Works (Not just one topic)

100-199   Philosophy

200-299   Religion

300-399   Social Science

400-499   Languages

500-599   Science

600-699   Useful Arts and Sciences

700-799   Fine Arts (art, hobbies, music, sports, etc.)

800-899   Literature (drama, poetry, etc.)

900-999   History, Travel, Biography

Part A. Read the titles of the books listed below. Write the Dewey number and category for each of the titles.

Example: *Dinosaurs*  500-599 Science

1. *The Colony of Rhode Island*
2. *Zoo Animals*
3. *The I Hate Mathematics Book*
4. *The Stitchery Book*
5. *Poems for Children*
6. *The Pooh Cookbook*
7. *In Other Words*
8. *The World Book Encyclopedia*
9. *Weather*
10. *The Easy Baseball Book*

Part B. Put the following numbers in numerical order.

| Set one: | 289 | 917 | 292 |
|---|---|---|---|
| | 636.6 | 424 | 636.1 |
| | 398.2 | 031 | 105.2 |
| | 105 | 920 | 398.6 |
| Set two: | 626.11 | 625.28 | 626.6 |
| | 624.6 | 626.3 | 627.1 |
| | 626.4 | 626.16 | 624.41 |

**Search and Found**

Now that you know how to use the card catalog and know how materials are organized in the library media center, you will practice finding materials using that knowledge.

Use the card catalog!!!!! As you find each material, have the library media specialist initial your paper showing that you have found it. Then replace the material where you found it!!!!!

1. Find a book by C. B. Colby.

2. Find a book by Eleanor Estes.

3. Find a book about an animal.

4. Find a biography about a famous man.

5. Find a KIT about Maryland.

6. Find a filmstrip about a planet.

7. Find a December issue of *Cricket* magazine.

8. Find an EASY book about an animal that you could read to a little brother or sister.

9. Find the book *High King.*

10. Find something in the vertical file about Maryland.

11. Find a book about one of the western states.

12. Find a poetry book.

13. Find an atlas.

14. Find an almanac.

15. Find a fiction book about a horse.

16. Find a record that is a folktale.

17. Find a chart that is about birds.

*Answer Sheet for Search and Find Unit*

**Organizational Patterns**

Students will explain the organizational patterns of:

1. Easy books
2. Fiction books
3. Nonfiction books
4. Periodicals
5. Vertical file
6. Kits
7. Filmstrips
8. Records
9. Charts
10. Biographies
11. Reference collection

**Card Catalog—The Keys to the Library Media Center**

1-9. yes
10. no

**Call Number—The Address of a Book or Material**

1-5. Answers depend on how the library media center is organized.
6. before
7. Record
8. Kit
9. The first letter of the author's last name.

**The Dewey Decimal System**

Part A

1. 900-999    History, Travel, Biography
2. 600-699    Useful Arts and Sciences
3. 500-599    Science
4. 700-799    Fine Arts
5. 800-899    Literature
6. 700-799    Fine Arts
7. 400-499    Languages
8. 000-099    General Works
9. 500-599    Science
10. 700-799   Fine Arts

Part B

| Set one: | 031 | 398.6 |
|---|---|---|
| | 105 | 424 |
| | 105.2 | 636.1 |
| | 289 | 636.6 |
| | 292 | 917 |
| | 398.2 | 920 |

| Set two: | 624.41 | 626.3 |
|---|---|---|
| | 624.6 | 626.4 |
| | 625.28 | 626.6 |
| | 626.11 | 627.1 |
| | 626.16 | |

**Search and Found**

Students will bring:

1. Book by C. B. Colby
2. Book by Eleanor Estes
3. Book about an animal
4. Biography of a woman
5. Kit about Maryland
6. Filmstrip about a planet
7. December issue of *Cricket* magazine
8. Easy book
9. *High King*
10. Something from the vertical file on Maryland
11. Book about one of the western states.
12. Poetry book
13. Atlas
14. Almanac
15. Fiction book about a horse
16. Folktale record
17. Chart about birds

# *Index*

Administrators, 66. *See also* Principal
Alphabetizing skills, 16-17
Art, use of, 58
Assessment, 3, 16, 32, 45-46, 48-49
    construction of, 16
    criterion-referenced, 16
    examples of, 39, 88, 91, 102, 103, 117, 134, 138
    general principles, 66
    identification of student strengths and deficiencies,
        17, 65
    of instruction, 31, 66
    of instructional materials, 4, 31, 32, 67-68
    of instructional program, 3, 4
    by observation, 65
    of student learning, 31, 45, 65-66
Authors and illustrators, 62-63
    lessons related to, 92-102

Booklets, use of. *See* Lap packs

Card catalog, lessons related to, 137-44
Catalog cards. *See* Card catalog
Characters, lessons related to, 92-102
Composition, use of, 59-60
Comprehension skills, lessons related to, 125-35
Curriculum
    integration of library media skills into, 3, 7, 31,
        58-61, 63, 117, 137
    examples of, 116-24

Demonstration method of instruction, 32, 37-39
Dictionaries, lessons related to, 103-15
Discussion method of instruction, 32, 46, 60
    examples, 125-34
Drama, use of, 58

Encyclopedias, lessons related to, 116-24
Evaluation. *See* Assessment
Every pupil response, 32, 46-49

Fable, 61
Facilities (school), variable related to, 32
Fantasy, 61
Fiction, 61
Folktales, 61

Game method of instruction, 32, 40-41
Goals. *See* Objectives
Group discussion. *See* Discussion method of
    instruction
Grouping of students, 32-34, 41
    examples, 10, 12, 32
    variables related to, 32
Guide words, lessons related to, 106-8

Identification skills, K-3 sequence, 18-23
Illustrations. *See* Authors and illustrators